DEMONSTRATIONS

OF

THE SPIRIT

RESTORED

Paul M Hanssen

SEVEN PILLARS CHURCH

COMMUNICATIONS

Email: contact@sevenpillarschurch.com

Web Site: www.sevenpillarschurch.com

Cover Design: Andrew L. Hanssen

Creative Leif Designs

creativeleif.com

Editor: Gwen D. Hanssen

Printed in the USA

Table of Contents

Introduction

Restoration

God's people today are privileged above every other generation that has been before. We are living in the last days before the soon return of our Savior, eternal King, and Heavenly Bridegroom, Jesus Christ. The Word of God informs us that the last days will be days of great restoration.

"Repent ye therefore, and be converted, that your sins may be blotted out, when the times of refreshing shall come from the presence of the Lord; And he shall send Jesus Christ, which before was preached unto you: Whom the heaven must receive (get hold of, attain, hold) until the times of restitution of all things, which God hath spoken by the mouth of all his holy prophets since the world began." (Acts 3:19-21)

These verses are taken from Peter's message to his Jewish brethren on the day that he and John went to the temple. There, a lame man was healed through Peter. In this great sermon, Peter taught about repentance, conversion and having sins blotted out in preparation for the times of refreshing (revival, recovery of breath, relieve) that had been promised would come from God in the last days. It is interesting to note that the Apostle Peter stated that the heaven must receive, or hold, Jesus until this refreshing or awakening has taken place and all things have been restored that had been spoken of by the prophets. These verses relate both to the natural Jewish nation as well as to the spiritual Jews, or the church.

The New Testament church was established on the new covenant and founded on the *Truth*. (Ephesians 2:19-22). It was built upon the sure foundation of God's Word, order, power and authority. The church was built on holiness, true liberty in the Spirit, the manifestations of the power of God, and upon God's divine infinite moral laws and principles. Through the centuries the church has lost many of these qualities. They have been replaced by man's plans and by man's order of performance.

Before Jesus returns, God's purpose and plan will once again be restored to His church as they were in the days of the Apostles. The end will be like the beginning! God's way of doing things will be revived. Those wanting to press on in God will once again awaken to the importance of falling in line with the Holy Scriptures.

We live in the lukewarm Laodicean church age where the vast majority of the religious world and mainstream

Christianity has adopted the self-satisfied, self-centered, dead and lethargic spirit of this present day. (Revelation 3:14-29)

I once heard a preacher say: *"The altar was once a place of sacrifice and repentance, but it has now become a stage of performance and entertainment"*. I could not agree more. At one point, the church used to call sinners to repentance under the conviction of the Holy Ghost. Now, however, the church puts on a stage show. *Church* has become a place of performance, a theater, rather than a place of worship. Many people go to the house of God to be entertained rather than be to have their lives changed.

Yet, in this lukewarm church era there are those who are constantly searching for Truth and yearning for a deeper and a closer more satisfying relationship with God. Christ Jesus gave a powerful beckoning call to this church age through the Apostle John.

"I counsel thee to buy of me gold tried in the fire, that thou mayest be rich; and white raiment, that thou mayest be clothed, and that the shame of thy nakedness do not appear; and anoint thine eyes with eyesalve, that thou mayest see." (Revelation 3:18)

Having our eyes anointed with the anointing oil of the Spirit of God will cause the scales of blindness and pride to fall off of our eyes so that we may truly have enlightened vision. Once our eyes are opened again, we will be able to see the condition of our churches as well as get a clearer vision of our personal spiritual lives. My prayer is that our eyes will be opened to the need for genuine repentance and brokenness. Then and only then will we clearly see the direction in which the cloud and fire of God's Holy Ghost is leading the church today. It is a time of restoration. It is time to wake up!

And that, knowing the time, that now it is high time to awake out of sleep: for now is our salvation nearer than when we believed. (Romans 13:11)

I have often fellowshipped faithful *old-timers* who have witnessed great revivals in the past. These precious saints are eagerly waiting for a similar move of God to take place as they had once experienced. However, we will not only experience the former things that have been seen throughout the past century. We will also witness an entirely new thing. We have been promised not only the former rain but also the latter rain in the end times. This means that the church will not only witness again what has been. It will also be partakers of something new and fresh. The move of God witnessed in past centuries is only a drop in the ocean in comparison to the outpouring that the early church experienced after they received the Holy Ghost fire. At that time, the faithful one hundred and twenty in the upper room were endued with power from on high.

After two days will he revive us: in the third day he will raise us up, and we shall live in his sight. Then shall we know, if we follow on to know the Lord: his going forth is prepared as the morning; and he shall come unto us as the rain, as the latter and former rain unto the earth. (Hosea 6:2-3)

I believe that the end is going to be like the beginning. I also believe that the end time church will be a partaker of something that the early church did not have which is something new and fresh. At the end, we will once again see and experience the wind, fire, and sound that the early church witnessed in the beginning. Not only will the former rain come down, but the latter rain will fall as well. The former and latter rain will fall, not at separate times or seasons, but both will fall at once. What a season of the outpouring of God's Spirit we can look forward to.

The latter day move of God is going to be much different than what many expect. Because of that there will be great numbers of God's people who will reject this restoration. As a result, we will see the church follow where God is moving or go nowhere at all.

God will never allow Himself to be manipulated by those who seek their own pleasure and fulfillment. Rather, His ears will hear those who call upon Him with their whole heart. He will move upon those who seek His outpouring with a humble, repentant and broken heart. (Jeremiah 29:12-14)

(Deuteronomy 4:29, Hosea 10:12, Daniel 9:3)

"Be glad then, ye children of Zion, and rejoice in the LORD your God: for he hath given you the former rain moderately, and he will cause to come down for you the rain, the former rain, in the first month. And the floors shall be full of wheat, and the fats shall overflow with wine and oil. And I will restore to you the years that the locust hath eaten, the

*cankerworm, and the caterpillar, and the palmerworm, my
great army which I sent among you." (Joel 2:23-25)*

*Come, and let us return unto the Lord: for he hath torn, and
he will heal us; he hath smitten, and he will bind us up. After
two days will he revive us: in the third day he will raise us
up, and we shall live in his sight. Then shall we know, if we
follow on to know the Lord: his going forth is prepared as
the morning; and he shall come unto us as the rain, as the
latter and former rain unto the earth. (Hosea 6:1-3)*

What tremendous promise the church has been given by
the Spirit of God through the Prophets Joel and Haggai.
This is a promise of the restoration of those things that
God's people have lost through the ages. Take note that the
promise speaks of the former and the latter rains.

The word former in the Hebrew is *mowreh*, which means
the early rain. This word goes back to the root word
yowreh, which means sprinkling, autumnal shower and
first rain

The autumn showers are cleansing showers. They cleanse
away the fallen dead leaves of previous life. The autumn
showers cleanse away decaying matter and prepare the
earth for new growth that is yet to come. The autumn
showers or the *former rain* was also the rain that fell in the
seed-sowing season. In Palestine, the seeds were planted
in the fall and the crops were harvested in the spring, or
before the dry hot season appeared.

We need this former rain in our midst to cleanse away pre-
conceived ideas, the death and the darkness of our carnal

reasoning, the dead leaves of previous experiences that often faithfully hang around to bind us. "Forgetting those things which are behind and reaching forth unto those things which are before," was Paul's message to the Philippians in chapter three and verse thirteen.

We also need the former rain to prepare the ground of our hearts for the seed of God's Word that He wishes to give us in the time of restoration.

God also promised the *latter rain*. The word *latter* in Hebrew is *malqowsh,* and it means the *spring rain*. It also goes back to a root word meaning *latter growth*. The spring rain comes to ripen the harvest and to prepare the fruit of the trees and the fruit of the ground for use. Oh God, send the cleansing and ripening rain and restore unto us that which has been eaten away from us during the past generations.

In Joel chapter two, God mentions four creatures that have destroyed the increase and blessings of the LORD: the locust, the cankerworm, the caterpillar and the palmer-worm. All of these creatures have one thing in common; they devour and destroy vegetation or plant life.

"Tell ye your children of it, and let your children tell their children, and their children another generation. That which the palmerworm hath left hath the locust eaten; and that which the locust hath left hath the cankerworm eaten; and that which the cankerworm hath left hath the caterpillar eaten." (Joel 1:3-4)

God used these creatures and their natures as a picture of the army that He had sent among His people to eat away their increase. You might ask the question, "Why did God send these creatures and cause this to happen?" It is often in the times of increase, blessing, and prosperity that mankind becomes self confident and removes his dependency from God and places it on himself, or "in" self.

The greatest test that a human being can go through is not that of poverty and need but that of blessings, riches and prosperity. Success has been a stumbling block to many men and women of God throughout the ages. Wealth, honor, power and fame have destroyed more lives thoughout history than anything else. Experiencing poverty, on the other hand, is a time when many call on the LORD God for help and lean on Him for support. King David wrote, "The poor committeth himself unto thee." (Psalm 10:14) In the times of blessing, abundance, increase, and prosperity, it is so easy to become self-confident and independent and place one's trust in wealth rather than in the Almighty Name and the providing hand of the LORD.

"The righteous also shall see, and fear, and shall laugh at him: Lo, this is the man that made not God his strength; but trusted in the abundance of his riches..." (Psalm 52:6-7)

Herein stands the reason that God sent the great army of devourers. His ultimate purpose was not to destroy His own people, but rather to cause them to see their own need for God even in times of great increase. There are very few in this world that attribute the blessings in their lives to God. Yet, in the time of pain and suffering, mankind will either turn to Him or damn and reject Him. In pain and suffering, God most frequently comes in view in some way.

" ...when your gardens and your vineyards and your fig trees and your olive trees increased, the palmerworm devoured them: yet have ye not returned unto me, saith the LORD." (Amos 4:9)

"He gave also their increase unto the caterpillar, and their labour unto the locust." (Psalm 78:46)

Down through the years, God, in His mercy, has blessed His people with both natural and spiritual increase. Due to this, many hearts have been lifted up in pride and self-confidence. Wealth has become a major focus in the church today. Large elaborate buildings called churches are the new idol of the day. Many people will not even enter a church unless it is of top design with the best of everything. God's people have become spoiled through the blessings that God has bestowed upon them. Instead of the blessings turning us to God, they have, in fact, turned us away from God. Therefore, He has permitted and ordained a devouring, as it were, of the spiritual increase in order that His people may turn their faces back to Him and recognize that if the LORD does not build the house then they who build labor in vain. We are nothing and can accomplish nothing without Him. (Psalm 127:1)

In my travels over the years to more than 70 countries, I have often been asked these questions: "Where is the blessing and the life that we once knew?" "Where has the power and the anointing gone that breaks yokes?" "Where is the progressive revelation and the unfolding of the

Word of God?" "Where is the Glory of God?" "Where are the true signs, wonders and miracles?" One answer to these questions is that for the most part these things have been *devoured.* God has ordained it in order to cause His people to turn away from the self-satisfied, self centered and self-dependent attitude that dominates the church world. There is a call for us to prepare for the times of refreshing and restoration that God so desires to bring to His church in His own way, in His own time and according to His own will. He is knocking on the doors of the hearts of His people. He is screaming with a loud voice through His Spirit, *"He that hath an ear, let him hear what the Spirit saith unto the churches." (Revelation 2:7)* What great days we live in!

"Who is left among you that saw this house in her first glory? and how do ye see it now? is it not in your eyes in comparison of it as nothing?" (Haggai 2:3)

To compare the greatness and glory of the beginning of the New Testament church with the church of today is of no comparison. Yet, we are encouraged in verse four of the same chapter in Haggai:

"...and be strong, all ye people of the land, saith the LORD, and work: *for I am with you, saith the LORD of hosts: "(Haggai 2:4)*

If we follow God's master plan and fulfill his divine will, the following will be the speedy result:

"THE GLORY OF THIS LATTER HOUSE SHALL BE GREATER THAN OF THE FORMER, SAITH THE LORD OF HOSTS: AND

IN THIS PLACE WILL I GIVE PEACE, SAITH THE LORD OF HOSTS."(Haggai2:9)

Chapter One

WHY
DEMONSTRATE

"And my speech and my preaching was not with enticing words of man's wisdom, but in demonstration of the Spirit and of power." (1 Corinthians 2:4)

This book is a study into one of the areas within the body of Christ that has been devoured, lost, rejected and/or thrown out of the church for the most part. In these last days, God wishes to restore the demonstrations of the Spirit to His church. Read the following chapters with an open mind and heart and allow the Spirit of God to enlighten your eyes to see the importance of *demonstrations of worship, or manifestations of the Spirit.*

The Apostle Paul made it clear to the Corinthians that he did not come to simply preach enticing words of man's wisdom. He did not come to bring knowledge without power. His aim was not to give an eloquent speech or a theological discourse. Rather, Paul gave the Word of God that was accompanied by and entangled in the demonstrative power of the Holy Ghost. The preaching of Paul demonstrated God's presence and power.

What does it mean to *demonstrate God's presence and power?* God's Spirit is often likened to the wind. The wind can be felt and even heard, but it cannot be seen. Well, actually, it can't be seen on it's own. Have you ever been sitting outside in the calm of the day and all of a sudden heard the wind coming your way bustling through the leaves of the trees and the grass of the field? Then, it hit you, the cool breeze swept over your body. You could not see the actual wind itself, but you felt it. You could also see the various ways that the wind was moving by watching the effect it had on the visible plant life surrounding you. You could see the trees swaying and the grass moving in all directions as the wind blew and they swirled freely. A pile of leaves can often be seen swirling around on the ground as if they were living, breathing and dancing in displays of joyful praise. It is not uncommon to see stray objects ascending, descending, up and down, twirling, and scooting along the ground as if they were living creatures. The invisible wind has the power to move these visible objects. It is through this display of the animate meeting the inanimate that we can "see" the wind, as it were.

In like manner, we feel, see and experience the Spirit of God. The Spirit is like the wind and we, His people, are like the trees that manifest a visible demonstration of the invisible movements of God's Spirit as He blows and moves upon us. Isaiah, the prophet, wrote that God's people are as trees of righteousness, the planting of the LORD. (Isaiah 61:3) The early church experienced the wind of the Holy Ghost in the upper room on the day of Pentecost. The saints were like trees that yielded their branches and leaves to the movement of the breath of God

18

as they outwardly demonstrated the touch of the rushing mighty wind blowing on them.

"And when the day of Pentecost was fully come, they were all with one accord in one place. And suddenly there came a sound from heaven as of a rushing mighty wind, and it filled all the house where they were sitting. And there appeared unto them cloven tongues like as of fire, and it sat upon each of them. And they were filled with the Holy Ghost, and began to speak with other tongues, as the Spirit gave them utterance... And they were all amazed, and were in doubt, saying one to another, What meaneth this? Others mocking said, These men are full of new wine." (Acts 2:1-4, 12-13)

I have often wondered what really must have taken place in the upper room on that glorious occasion when God fulfilled His promise and sent the Holy Ghost. Something quite dramatic, apart from the one hundred and twenty speaking in tongues, must have been happening that day. Many heard and saw the commotion and began supposing that the people in the upper room were drunk. As the invisible rushing wind of the Spirit moved on those gathered, they demonstrated the invisible move of the Holy Ghost with praise, worship, noise, prayer and new tongues.

The reason that this scene from the early church is rarely seen in the present day church is due to the fact that the church has become hardened and insensitive to the Spirit of God. We are unmoved when the *wind* blows. Our pride, our programs and our longing to please the multitude has caused us to move the way that man wants us to move, rather than the way that God wants us to move. We also carry a fear of what people will say and think about us. The church continues to compromise and form itself according to this humanistic way of thinking of the present day. We fear the loss of our congregations should we welcome the move of God's Spirit. Our church services have become places of comfort, rather than a place of conviction.

The church needs to be restored in order to allow God to move according to His Word and according to the leading of His Spirit. We often voice our desire to have the mantles of the prophets of old in our midst. We want the power and the anointing of the New Testament apostles. However, to possess such power and anointing, we must be willing to pay the same price that they paid. Many want the anointing of the men of old, yet few want to become a crushed olive so as to release the flow of the anointing oil. The men and the woman of old walked in brokenness, humility, obedience, and surrender. They were fearless towards people's thoughts, words, attacks and opposition. They did not compromise, but they stood on and for Truth no matter the cost.

Unfortunately, man has become wise in his own eyes. The wisdom of man is quite contrary to the wisdom of God. Because of the man-made wisdom that dominates the church world, the simplicity within God's house has all but gone down the drain. The power and the effect of the demonstrations of the Spirit in our prayer, praise and worship are very rarely accepted, because to the carnal mind of man they appear foolish and in the eyes of the so-called wise they appear to lack good sense.

For it is written, I will destroy the wisdom of the wise, and will bring to nothing the understanding of the prudent... For ye see your calling brethren, how that not many wise men after the flesh, not many mighty, not many noble, are called: But God hath chosen the foolish things of the world to confound the wise; and God hath chosen the weak things of the world to confound the things which are mighty; And base things of the world, and things which are despised, hath God chosen, yea, and things which are not, to bring to nought things that are: That no flesh should glory in his presence. (1 Corinthians 1:19, 26-29)

God has always used things that seem foolish to the carnal mind to demonstrate His power and glory. He uses that which is contrary to the thoughts of man to bring His will to birth. Who would have thought it wise to build a boat, on a mountain nonetheless, in a place that had no water and where it had never rained before? Yet, this is what God commanded Noah to do. God's wisdom was foolishness to man, yet God's wisdom was man's redemption. God has not changed. The problem is, however, that we, the church, have changed. As worldly knowledge has increased, mankind has become increasingly wiser in his own thinking. But, God has promised to destroy man's wisdom. The wisdom of this world is foolishness in the eyes of God because it is vain, proud and void of Godly understanding.

Let no man deceive himself. If any man among you seemeth to be wise in this world, let him become a fool, that he may be wise. For the wisdom of this world is foolishness with God. For it is written, He taketh the wise in their own craftiness.

And again, The Lord knoweth the thoughts of the wise, that they are vain. (1 Corinthians 3:18-20)

Notice, in the verse above it says, "*if any man among you seemeth to be wise in the world, let him become a fool.*" This verse did not say, "Let him become foolish," but rather it said, "Let him become a fool." This word, fool, in the Greek, comes from the word *musterion*, which means to shut the mouth. We open our mouths so often out of ignorance and we speak words that we deem as wise and knowledgeable. Instead, God wants us to shut our mouths and therewith express wisdom. As a result, we can be taught the Truth and become wise with the wisdom, understanding and knowledge of God. Do not speak about things that you do not know anything about. Keep your mouth shut, be wise and learn. Proverbs chapter seventeen and verse twenty-eight states, "*Even a fool, when he holdeth his peace, is counted wise: and he that shutteth his lips is esteemed a man of understanding.*"

Paul the Apostle's ministry was not based on the wisdom of man's words.

And my speech and my preaching was not with enticing words of man's wisdom, but in demonstration of the Spirit and of power: that your faith should not stand in the wisdom of men, but in the power of God. (1 Corinthians 2:4-5)

For our gospel came not unto you in word only, but also in power and in the Holy Ghost, and in much assurance; as ye know what manner of men we were among you for your sake. (1 Thessalonians 1:5)

The demonstrations of the Spirit will sanctify the believer from the vain and proud thoughts of the carnal mind. The demonstrations of the Spirit set mankind free from the bondage of the *self* to serve the living God according to the move and flow of His Spirit and His divine will.

The word, *demonstrate*, means to show off, exhibit, demonstrate, accredit, prove, set forth, shew, and manifest.

The raising of the hands, the clapping of the hands and being slain in the Spirit, or falling prostrate, are demonstrations that are widely accepted in the mainstream church world today. However, God's Word speaks of many more demonstrations that the church has rejected and conveniently gotten rid of due to what it has cost the church to yield to the move of God's Spirit. Many forms of demonstrative expression have been abandoned.

God wants to set His people free and reveal Himself as He did in the days of old. Even as He did on Mount Sinai, so God wants to manifest Himself again through His Spirit and Word. However, for God to manifest Himself in such a manner, God's people must be willing to become yielded vessels to the moving of *the wind*, so to speak. Then, instead of becoming hindrances to the move of the breath of God, we can become channels through whom the Spirit of God can flow.

Demonstrations are visible manifestations of the moving of God's invisible Spirit and power. When a person yields to the power of God's Spirit, it sanctifies the channels of man's being while manifesting great spiritual mysteries.

CHAPTER TWO

CLAPPING

Clapping is one of the most accepted forms of the demonstrations of praise in many churches today. Regardless, very few really understand the spiritual significance and the meaning of the clapping of the hands. Many do not know the power and the spiritual significance of this simple act of praise. Many do not consider what is put into motion when they clap their two hands, with their ten fingers, together. The clap, as well as any other form of demonstrative praise and worship, becomes far more effective and powerful when the worshipper understands what he or she is doing. Great faith arises when we grasp the impact that our demonstration is having in our own personal life, as well as the impact that is taking place in the invisible heavenly realms and spirit world.

The Bible has not been given to us as a history book or as a theological manual. Rather, it has been given to us as a *guidebook* as we endeavor to grow into the measure of the stature of the fullness of Christ (Ephesians 4:11-15.) We have to follow the guidebook as it is a map that will lead us back into the union and relationship that man had with God in the beginning and that God desires to have with mankind again.

All scripture is given by inspiration of God, and is profitable for doctrine, for reproof, for correction, for instruction in righteousness: that the man of God may be perfect, thoroughly furnished unto all good works. (2 Timothy 3; 16-17)

Before examining the principles in God's Word about clapping, let us pause for a moment and establish some basic truths needed for our understanding.

Take note in the above verse where it states, "A*ll scripture is* given by inspiration of God, and *is* profitable." The word "is" is the key word. God's Word *IS* given, and it *IS* profitable today for my learning. Some teach that only portions of scripture are for today's generation. This could not be further from the Truth.

Many believers divide the Word of God into different dispensations, and remove whatever suits them or does not fit into their particular theology. There is then a labeling of each divided portion as "Word for this age" or "Word for a past age". However, the Bible, from Genesis to Revelation, *is*, present tense, profitable to me for doctrine, reproof, correction and instruction.

There are multitudes of believers who do not accept that the Old Testament is for the New Testament child of God. This is false and contrary to the scriptures.

For whatsoever things were written aforetime were written for our learning, that we through patience and comfort of the scriptures must have hope. (Romans 15:4)

Because of the fact that a great portion of this study is taken from the Old Testament scriptures, we must realize and understand that the Old Testament was written for our learning. God recorded natural accounts in the Old Testament and revealed spiritual principles and laws of the way in which He moves and operates. He still works today as He did yesterday. He remains a never changing God.

Now all these things happened unto them for ensamples: and they are written for our admonition, upon whom the ends of the world are come. (1 Corinthians 10:11)

Speaking about the journey of the Israelites from Egypt to Canaan's land and everything that happened to them on the journey and beyond, the Apostle Paul said, under the inspiration of God's Spirit, that it all happened to them for our ensample or example. The nation of Israel experienced many things in the natural realm that God has graciously revealed to us for spiritual reasons and purposes. Israel's natural pilgrimage is a mirror reflection of our spiritual pilgrimage.

Paul also believed in God's moral law and divine principles that were written in the Law and were written by the prophets.

But this I confess unto thee, that after the way which they call heresy, so worship I the God of my fathers, believing all things which are written in the law and in the prophets: (Acts 24:14)

Paul not only believed the writings of old, but he also preached about Jesus from the Old Testament.

And when they had appointed him a day, there came many to him into his lodging; to whom he expounded and testified the kingdom of God, persuading them concerning Jesus, **both out of the law of Moses, and out of the prophets,** *from morning to evening. (Acts 28:23)*

Jesus preached from Moses' writings concerning Himself.

For had ye believed Moses, ye would have believed me: for **he wrote of me.** *But if ye believe not his writings, how shall ye believe my words? (John 5:46-47)*

(See other New Testament scriptures revealing the validity of the Old Testament for this generation: Acts 26:22; Luke 24:27; Romans 15:4; 1 Corinthians 10:11)

The Old Testament occupies three-quarters of God's Word. It behooves us to examine it and to learn the spiritual principles and tremendous treasures that God has laid up for us in this great portion of scripture. Many have said said concerning the two testaments: *"The old is in the new revealed and the new is in the old concealed."*

There are many areas of the New Testament that you will never understand until you begin to see and understand God's great moral laws and spiritual principles given to us in the Old Testament. Having then this truth established, let us proceed with the demonstration of clapping.

CLAPPING OF THE HANDS

It is most interesting to note that the clapping of the hands is never mentioned in the New Testament. As a matter of fact, it is only ever mentioned, in one form or another, about nine times throughout the Old Testament. Yet, there is more than enough evidence to show us that God wants His holy Name lifted up with *the clap*.

O clap your hands, all ye people; shout unto God with the voice of triumph. (Psalm 47:1)

Clapping of the hands and shouting with the voice of triumph go hand in hand. First and foremost, clapping is a demonstration of victory. Not only does it demonstrate the success of the victor, but it also puts down and despises the opponent. We only have to look in the natural realm to understand this principle in the spiritual realm.

When sports fans attend a competition of any kind and their favorite team scores a goal or takes the lead, the natural response is that the supporters clap and shout for the success or victory of their team. As a result, the same clap and shout that lifts up and exalts the victor puts down and discourages the opponent or losing team.

A. Clap to celebrate the Triumph of Our God (Coronation)

And he brought forth the king's son, and put the crown upon him, and gave him the testimony; and they made him king, and anointed him; and they clapped their hands, and said, God save the king. (2 Kings 11:12)

29

The above verse is a natural, prophetic picture of Jesus being made king and placed on the throne as the triumphant victor. Ahaziah was king of Judea in those days and he had a wicked mother called Athaliah. When King Ahaziah died, his mother desired to possess the throne and govern the nation. Hence, she decided to destroy all of the royal seed of her son. Her attempt failed when Jehosheba, sister to King Ahaziah, took Joash (King Ahaziah's youngest son) and hid him in the house of the LORD for six years.

After that period of time, Joash was brought out of the LORD'S house and was made king and the wicked reign of Athaliah was overthrown.

What a beautiful picture of the triumph of our Lord Jesus. The enemy has tried to destroy the royal seed but the seed was spared. He lives forever more. He now sits on the throne.

The name *Jehosheba* in Hebrew actually means *Jehovah sworn, be safe, free, succour, defend, preserve, avenge, deliver, rescue and salvation.* When Jesus died, He had a promise from God, the Father, that He would not leave His soul in hell nor suffer, or allow, His Holy One to see corruption (Acts 2:27).

Jehovah had sworn salvation to His Son. God had sworn that the royal seed would come forth and take the throne of authority, government and all power.

We have the privilege, as the subjects of His kingdom, to demonstrate the victory of our King by clapping and putting Him on the throne. Whilst we place the King on His victorious throne in our own hearts, we are also demonstrating the putting down and destruction of the one who has been overcome or overthrown. The defeated one is our enemy called the dragon, serpent, devil and Satan. (Revelation 12:9).

B. Clap in Defeat of the Enemy or The Opponent (Derision or Scorn)

*And when Athaliah **heard the noise** of the guard and of the people, she came to the people into the temple of the LORD. And when she looked, behold, the king stood by a pillar, as the manner was, and the princes and the trumpeters by the king, and all the people of the land rejoiced, and blew with trumpets: and Athaliah rent her clothes, and cried, Treason, Treason. But Jehoiada the priest commanded the captains of the hundreds, the officers of the host, and said unto them, Have her forth without the ranges: and him that followeth her kill with the sword. For the priest had said, Let her not be slain in the house of the LORD. And they laid hands on her; and she went by the way by the which the horses came into the king's house: and there was she slain. (2 Kings 11:13-16)*

As the people clapped in triumph as their new King was placed on the throne, Athaliah's reign and government was despised, rejected, pulled down and came to an end. While the people clapped and shouted in triumph, Athaliah was taken out of the temple and slain. The clapping of hands honors and promotes the king of kings, and demotes and defames the enemy of our souls!

Behold, I am against thee, saith the LORD of hosts; and I will discover thy skirts upon thy face, and I will shew the nations thy nakedness, and the kingdoms thy shame... There is no healing of thy bruise; thy wound is grievous: all that hear the bruit of thee shall clap the hands *over thee: for upon whom hath not thy wickedness passed continually? (Nahum3: 5, 19)*

Thus saith the Lord God; Smite with thine hand, and stamp with thy foot, and say, Alas for all the evil abominations... (Ezekiel 6:ll)

The above verses are speaking about the wicked city of Nineveh. God was pronouncing His judgment upon her. It is stated; "*All that hear the bruit of thee shall clap the hands over thee*". The word bruit in Hebrew is *shema*. This word means *announcement, something heard, report, tidings*. In other words, this verse is revealing that all who hear the announcement or tidings of the judgment and destruction that God was sending upon Nineveh will clap their hands. We can clap our hands in triumph and victory over the wicked one who has been defeated by the cross of Calvary. We also clap our hands to exalt the One and the only true King, the LORD Jesus Christ, and place Him upon the throne of our hearts. What a powerful demonstration and act of worship!

TWO HANDS / TEN FINGERS

The word clap in Hebrew is *taga*, which means to *clatter, slap the hands together, clang*. It also means to *become a bondsman by hand clasping, smite, sound, strike and thrust*.

Take note of one of the meanings of clapping: **to become a bondsman by hand clasping**. To be a bondsman means to be united or bound to something. What is God showing us here? What do we become a bondsman to? What are we *bringing together*, as it were, as we clap our hands and what are we uniting ourselves with, or joining ourselves to?

When God created man, He formed man in His own image and likeness. (Genesis 1:26) Man was made with two hands; each hand having five fingers. We have, of course, a right hand and a left hand. God also has two hands; one right hand and one left hand. The right hand of God, according to scripture, speaks of exaltation or pleasure, while the left hand speaks of humility or pain.

    i.   God's Right Hand of Blessing

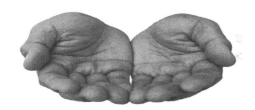

Right Hand/Exaltation   Left Hand /Humility

PLEASURE-BLESSING   PAIN -JUDGEMENT

Thou wilt shew me the path of life: in thy presence is fulness of joy; at thy right hand there are pleasures for evermore. (Psalm 16:11)

Thou hast a mighty arm: strong is thy hand, and high is thy right hand. *(Psalm 89:13)*

In Genesis, we see yet another story that shows us the principle of the right hand and the left hand of God.

And Joseph took them, Ephraim in his right hand toward Israel's left hand, and Manasseh in his left hand toward Israel's right hand, and brought them near unto him. (Genesis 48:13)

ISRAEL

Right Hand   Left Hand

Manasseh – First Born   Ephraim – Second Born

JOSEPH

And Israel stretched out his right hand, laid it upon Ephraim's head, who was the younger, and his left hand upon Manasseh's head, guiding his hands wittingly; for Manasseh was the firstborn. (Genesis 48:13-14)

And when Joseph saw that his father laid his right hand upon the head of Ephraim, it displeased him: and he held up his father's hand, to remove it from Ephraim's head unto Manasseh's head.

And Joseph said unto his father, Not so my father: for this is the firstborn; put thy right hand upon his head. And his father refused, and said, I know it, my son, I know it: he also shall become a people, and he also shall be great: but truly his younger brother shall be greater than he, and his seed shall become a multitude of nations. (Genesis 48:17-19)

The right hand of the exalted blessing always belonged to the firstborn. In this instance, Israel crossed his hands and placed the blessing of multiplication, pleasure and exaltation on the head of Ephraim, the second born. He then placed his left hand on the head of Manasseh, the firstborn, and gave him the humility blessing.

ii.   God's Left Hand of Pain

The LORD is a God of perfect balance. He created everything with his own Word. His Word reveals His nature. All things were created in balance. For example: seed time and harvest, cold and hot, summer and winter, day and night, pleasure and pain, mountains and valleys, noise and silence, male and female, and on and on the list goes. (Genesis 8:22).

Everything that proceeds from the mouth of God, or from His Word, comes in perfect balance: hailstones and coals of fire (Psalm 18:13). He made heights and depths, light and darkness, peace and evil - (misery, woe, affliction, calamity) – (Isaiah 45:6-7). God created up and down, left and right, pleasure and pain, judgment and blessing. These things have their origin in the perfect balanced nature of God and they are related to the right and to the left hand principle. Let us take a look at some scriptures that will help to enlighten our eyes on God's left hand of humility, pain and judgment.

The story that we will look at in the verses below starts with the children of Israel having done evil in the sight of the LORD. God, therefore, caused King Eglon of Moab to be strengthened and to overtake Israel. Eglon occupied the cities in Israel and the nation served Eglon for eighteen long years.

The time came in God's plan for Israel to be delivered. The people cried unto the LORD their God:

But when the children of Israel cried unto the LORD, the LORD raised them up a deliverer, Ehud the son of Gera, a Benjamite, a man **left handed:** *and by him the children of Israel sent a present unto Eglon the king of Moab....But Ehud made him a dagger which had two edges, of a cubit length; and he did gird it under his raiment upon his right thigh. And he brought the present unto Eglon king of Moab:...And Ehud came unto him; and he was sitting in a summer parlour, which he had for himself alone. And Ehud said, I have* a *message from God unto thee. And he arose from out of his seat. And Ehud put forth his* left *hand, and took the*

dagger from his right thigh, and thrust it into his belly.
(Judges 3:15-16, 20-21)

We must remember that all scripture is inspired and *is* profitable for us today. The verses above are full of divine Truth and spiritual principles. It is interesting to note that God chose a left-handed man for this particular purpose. There is no such thing as chance or coincidence with God. Everything has a cause, a plan and a purpose. God chose a left-handed man to execute judgment with a two-edged sword. Ehud told King Eglon that he had a message to him *from God*. The message was the drawn sword in the left hand of humility. Because of this, pain and judgment were thrust into his belly. The sword brought death to King Eglon as judgment from God.

Our Lord has always, and will always, operate by His divine laws. Now that we have briefly looked at the right and left hand of God, let us go back to the clapping of the hands.

When we clap before the LORD, we join our right and left hands together in union. As we all know, each of our hands has five fingers that together total ten fingers. Ten is the number of God's Law. The divine Law of God has both a blessing and judgment side. In other words, there is a right and a left hand. God's hand ministers blessing to those who obey His divine, moral laws. In contrast, His hand also ministers judgment to those who disobey.

Since the fall in the Garden of Eden mankind has been guilty of trying to administer the blessing and the judgment of God's Law according to his own fallen, human

reasoning. We dish out blessings to those whom we think are worthy and we are quick to judge and condemn those whom we feel are in need of judgment. We sway back and forth like the pendulum of a clock, from one side of the scales to the other. We give blessing and judgment as we see fit. Apart from God man does not know how to judge righteously. God is the only righteous judge and the only one who has the complete right and authority to judge....
for God is judge Himself. (Psalm 50:6)

...for thou shalt judge the people righteously, and govern the nations upon the earth. Selah. (Psalm 67:4)

When God judges, His judgments are always righteous, fair and just. He is the only one who can judge righteously because He alone sees and knows all things. Only He can see where a person is coming from, where they are in the present moment, and moreover where they are going. God always judges with the full picture in view. Man is not able to see the full picture of anyone's life, including his own. When God lifts up and promotes, or exalts with His right hand, His verdict or judgment is just. When He puts down, humbles or rebukes, His verdict and judgment is just.

But God is the judge, he putteth down one, and setteth up another. (Psalm 75:7)

God wants us to allow Him to be the judge and execute His judgments according to His knowledge, His will and His all viewing eye. We must learn to stand in the middle of God's scales (His perfect will) and become one, united, with His righteous judgments whether they be on the side of pleasure and exaltation or on the side of pain and humility.

As we bring our hands together and clap, we are first and foremost demonstrating becoming a bondsman with the righteous judgments of the LORD in our personal lives. As we acknowledge this in our own lives we are also able to acknowledge it in the lives of others, as well as in nature, in creation, and in the heavenly realms of the invisible spiritual world.

Judge not, and ye shall not be judged...(Luke 6:37)

We are not able to judge righteously. Therefore, we are cautioned not to judge. As a result, we can choose to allow Him to be who and what He is, which is the righteous Judge of all. As we clap our hands in faith, we can demonstrate bringing both sides of the Law together. We are becoming a bondsmen, as it were, to God's righteous verdicts. Our heart is saying, *"I accept your authority as the Just Judge and I unite myself to your righteous judgments."*

This is a tremendous principle to learn. Practicing this principle in our daily lives brings great peace to one's heart. Humankind are not capable of judging anything, this includes our own selves. Man has no ability to judge righteously.

iii.   The High and The Low

*For ye shall go out with joy, and be led forth with peace...and all the **trees** of the field shall **clap their hands**. (Isaiah 55:12)*

*Let the **floods clap their hands**. (Psalm 98:8)*

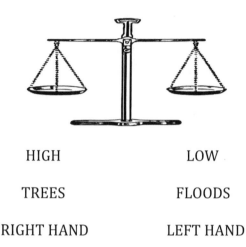

HIGH	LOW
TREES	FLOODS
RIGHT HAND	LEFT HAND

The trees demonstrate their movement or the clapping of their hands (leaves and branches) as the wind moves in and through the high place. In contrast, the floods move and demonstrate the clapping of their hands (waves) as the wind moves in the low places. Here, once again, we see the balance of God's right and left hand. This is symbolic of the high and the low, or the opposites of His exalted and His humility nature.

May we too learn to be yielded vessels that are moved by the breath of God's Spirit whether it be under His hot exalted breath or under His cold breath of humility. Let us clap our hands in joy as we demonstrate our yielding in surrender to God's high and low movements of blessing and judgment, pleasure and pain, exaltation and humility, as He moves upon us by His Spirit.

Chapter Three

RAISED HANDS

3

The raising of the hands is a common and accepted demonstration of worship in many churches. Christian groups worldwide practice the raising of the hands in their services. One can walk into almost any charismatic, non-denominational Christian, Pentecostal, Baptist, and many other mainstream churches and witness parishioners raising their hands during worship services.

Let us consider what the Bible teaches us about this powerful act of worship.

A. Surrender

First of all, raised hands are an outward demonstration of the surrender and submission of one's heart and will to God.

"I will delight myself in thy commandments, which I have loved. My hands also will I lift up unto thy commandments, which I have loved; and I will meditate in thy statutes" *(Psalm 119:47-48).*

Here, King David was proclaiming his surrender to the commandments of God. Take note that David said that he would lift up his hands, plural, not hand, singular. God's divine authority is expressed in His commandments and in His great Name. God demands surrender to the authority of His divine Laws and to the workings of His Almighty Name.

"Thus will I bless thee while I live: I will lift up my hands *in thy name" (Psalm 63:4).*

In this passage of scripture, David is saying, "I will lift up my hands in surrender to the authority of your Name." It is the name of the LORD that is the cause, the source, the purpose and the reason of all things. He is the head over all things to His church. (Ephesians 1:22) All things are done and permitted for His Name's sake that the glory and the might of His eternal redemptive effect may be revealed. He saves mankind for His Name's sake. (Psalm 106:8). He leads us on for His Name's sake (Psalm 23:3) God quickens for His Name's sake. (Psalm 143:11) He works great deeds for His Name's sake. (Ezekiel 20:14) All things are for His Name's sake, or for the sake of His Name.

Knowing and understanding this principle helps us to lift our hands in surrender to the Name of the LORD God in all of life's circumstances. Apart from the words that we speak, almost everything that we do originates with the hands. Before we go somewhere, we put on shoes appropriate for our destiny or activity. We do so with our hands. We dress ourselves with our hands. We eat with our hands. We work with our hands. We touch with our hands. We build with our hands. We also destroy with our hands and hurt with our hands. We create with our hands. We write with our hands. We gesture with our hands. We play music with our hands. This list could go on and on. Is it, therefore, any wonder that it is the hands that are to be lifted in surrender to God's Commandments and in honor to His Holy Name? As we lift our hands in surrender to God, we are surrendering all that we do with our hands unto Him.

Yet, so often we come before the LORD with anger in our hearts towards Him, who is the cause, the source and the fountain from which all things originate. We doubt His dealings with us. We doubt that He is able to redeem us. Coming before Him with doubt and anger is not surrender to the will and to the purpose of God. Paul wrote to Timothy and said...

"I will therefore that men pray everywhere, lifting up holy hands, without wrath and doubting" (1 Timothy 2:8).

When surrendering to the headship and the authority of the name of the LORD we should do so with joy and faith, without wrath or doubting, knowing that He will have His way and God's master plan will be performed.

God accepts the offering of clean hands raised unto His Holy Name. Clean hands are hands that are cleansed of animosity, anger, accusation, doubt and distrust toward the holiness of God. Unclean hands that are raised in His presence will cause God to hide His eyes.

And when ye spread forth your hands, I will hide mine eyes from you: yea, when ye make many prayers, I will not hear: your hands are full of blood. Wash you, make you clean; put away the evil of your doings from before mine eyes; cease to do evil; (Isaiah 1:15-16)

The lifting of our hands must never mask our sin or the uncleanness of our hands. Rather, the raising of our hands should express our trust and surrender to the Name of the LORD.

B.   Lifting The Heart to God

Not only are raised hands a demonstration of surrender, but this powerful demonstration also speaks of the worshipper lifting the heart up unto God.

" Let us lift up our heart with our hands unto God in the heavens". (Lamentations 3:41)

The word for heart in Hebrew is *lay-bawb*, from the root word *labe,* meaning feelings, intellect, the center, the will, the mind and the understanding. These two words illustrate to us the meaning of what we are lifting up to the LORD as we raise our hands in worship unto Him. By faith, as we lift our hearts, by raising our hands, we are presenting our inner most feelings, our will, and even our intellectual mind and understanding, unto the LORD. We are expressing, "Here it is my LORD, the very center of me, the core of my being, the place that you have chosen to establish your throne. I lift it all unto you, take your place in my heart!"

C.   Pleading - Supplication

The raising of the hands also has to do with pleading and supplicating towards God.

Hear the voice of my supplications, when I cry unto thee, when I lift up my hands toward thy holy oracle. (Psalm 28:2)

The heart of a parent is moved when the little son or the little daughter comes with stretched out hands pleading to be picked up and held. If human beings can be moved by such a sight, then how much more is the heart of God moved when His children raise their hands to Him, pleading for strength, pleading for forgiveness, pleading for love, pleading to be picked up and to be held in the arms of the Heavenly Father?

Arise, cry out in the night: in the beginning of the watches pour out thine heart like water before the face of the Lord: lift up thy hands toward him for the life of thy young children, that faint for hunger in the top of every street. (Lamentations 2:19)

Our God is merciful, kind and full of compassion. What a thrill it is to come before Him in our poverty and in our weakness and to have Him pick us up and embrace us as we stretch forth and lift up our hands in supplication.

I stretch forth my hands unto thee: my soul thirsteth after thee, as a thirsty land. Selah. (Psalm 143:6)

David craved God and His presence. He raised his hands toward the living God as his soul pleaded for a drink, as it were, of the fresh waters of the presence of Yaweh.

God responds to such thirst. He pours out His rain upon those who express their hunger and thirst for Him.

D. Praise – Blessing - Thanksgiving

The raising of the hands is also a demonstration of praising and blessing the LORD, or of lifting up His Name.

Lift up your hands in the sanctuary, and bless the LORD. (Psalm 134:2)

The Name of the LORD Jesus is the one name worthy to be lifted up. The world curses and mocks this beautiful Name. The Name of Jesus is used as a common curse word. But, God's people have the responsibility to pick up His Holy Name out of the dust of this world where it is trodden down and lift it up.

Let us come before His presence with thanksgiving; Let us shout joyfully to Him with psalms" (Psalm 95:2)

The word for thanksgiving is *to-dah* from the root word yaw-daw. It means to hold out the hand, an extension of the hand, especially to revere or worship with extended hands and a sacrifice of praise. It is to thank and praise God with one's hands extended whilst offering confession.

E. Warfare

The raising of the hands may be the simplest and seemingly most insignificant act of worship. However, when our hands are raised in faith and with surrender, while presenting our hearts with pleading, blessing and thanksgiving, the heavens begin to shake which causes havoc in the realms of spiritual warfare.

And it came to pass, when Moses held up his hand, that Israel prevailed: and when he let down his hand, Amalek prevailed. (Exodus 17:11)

Moses went up to the mount with Aaron, the high priest, and Hur, who came from the tribe of Judah. Judah means praise. It was Aaron and Hur that stayed Moses' arms when they were heavy (vs 10-12). Priestly worship will win the war. Lift up the hands with priestly worship with the rod of God extended, or the Name of the LORD lifted up. Victory will be the speedy result in the camp of God's people.

Chapter Four

DANCING

A time to weep, and a time to laugh, a time to mourn, and a time to dance; *(Ecclesiastes 3:4)*

God's people were the first ones to ever dance. God was the originator and the creator of the dance. He gave this freedom of expression to His people for them to use it as a form of demonstrative worship and adoration to His Holy Name. The devil has stolen and perverted this expression just as he has stolen everything that he uses. All of fallen Lucifer's possessions and all that is in the world today have their origin in God. The devil cannot create. The devil only steals and perverts what he possesses and uses.

The thief cometh not, but for to steal, *and to kill, and to* destroy... *(John 10:10)*

The very power that the devil possesses has its source in God. God created Lucifer as the cherub to cover and protect the throne of God.

Thou art the anointed cherub that covereth; and I have set thee so... (Ezekiel 28:14)

Cherubim are angelic beings with a tremendous God given power to fight and to wage war. Lucifer had the responsibility to guard the righteousness and the holiness of the throne of God and His divine Law. Lucifer was created with music within him as a means of power to help him fulfill his calling and responsibility.

... the workmanship of thy tabrets *and of thy* pipes *was prepared in thee in the day that thou wast created. (Ezekiel 28:13)*

MUSIC

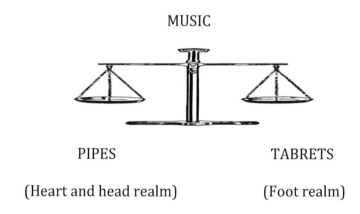

PIPES   TABRETS

(Heart and head realm)   (Foot realm)

Here, in Lucifer himself, we see God's balance in the music realm. The *tabrets* speak of the form of music that carry and create a beat, or rhythm, which move the feet. The *pipes* speak of the realm of music that moves the heart and the head, or the intellect. This realm of music releases the fountains of the head, stirring the emotions of one's inner being and soothes the soul.

When Lucifer fell from his exalted position, he took the power of music with him and perverted this great gift. He has used these perverted forms of music ever since for his own benefit and for the building of his wicked kingdom. Nevertheless, God has always intended that this *power* belong to His people. He has purposed for music to be used in the house of God in worship and for spiritual warfare.

King David possessed this power. His music, even though it was worship to God, was also a weapon of war. When he played his anointed music in the presence of King Saul who was troubled by evil spirits, Saul was liberated as the music warred, as it were, and drove back the powers that plagued him. (1 Samuel 16:23)

We need to rise up and take back what rightfully belongs to us by sanctifying it and by bringing the use of music in line with God's Word. We need to use the *tabrets and the pipes* for the glory of our God. Music releases tremendous power in the realms of the spirit when ministered under the anointing of God's Spirit. Anointed music causes the wind of God's Spirit to blow. As a result, it will bring cleansing, life, healing, restoration, and revelation to be ministered in the house of God.

The *dance* is one form of worship that Lucifer stole. God's Word reveals what the dance was originally created for.

First of all, there is something that needs to be made absolutely clear. There are those who believe that only a selected group should dance. Some churches have "dance teams" trained in the art of dancing. This has led many in the church to become spectators and to relax in their personal worship to God. In this instance, the dance has been designated to only a chosen few. For example, the dancers will meet together to practice their techniques on certain nights of each week to fit with the new songs that flow into the church. On Sunday morning, the *performance* is given and many even call it *dancing in the Spirit.* The dancers are usually good looking with slim, athletic physiques. I have often visited churches where this type of "worship" takes place.

As the dancers step out and perform, people's attention is taken off of their personal worship and praise to the LORD and is placed on these graceful moving figures on the platform. Worship then becomes a stage performance rather than an active part of the congregation's expression of adoration to God. This is not scriptural and should not find place in the house of God. Dancing was never intended to be entertainment for observers nor was it meant for only a selected few.

In contrast, God intended for the whole nation of Israel to dance in victory, and in praise and gratitude to the LORD their God.

Let Israel rejoice in him that made him: let the children of Zion be joyful in their King. Let them praise his name in the dance: *let them sing praises unto them with the timbrel and harp. For the LORD taketh pleasure in his people: (Psalm 149:2-4)*

Praise him with the timbrel and dance... Let everything that hath breath praise the LORD. Praise ye the LORD. (Psalm 150:4,6)

If you are a part of spiritual Israel, if you have breath and strength or ability in the physical body, then God has called you to praise Him in the dance.

In most cases dancing is not a matter of "can I or can't I", but rather "will I or will I not". The dance is for all ages, and for all nationalities. It is not dependent on whether you are tall or short, fat or skinny, young or old, black or white.

*Then shall the **virgin rejoice in the dance, both** young **men and** old **together**: for I will turn their mourning into joy, and will comfort them, and make them rejoice from their sorrow. (Jeremiah 31:13)*

Another thing that needs clarification is the term "dance in the Spirit". How often have people used this term as an excuse not to dance? Many think that unless some uncontrollable force sweeps over them and causes them to dance like a professional ballerina, then they should not dance.

Christians today walk and operate by feelings instead of operating by faith and in obedience to God's Word. Dancing, just like any other form of worship, such as singing, raising hands and clapping, is an act of the will in obedience to God's laws of praise.

The only stipulation or condition concerning dancing given in the scriptures is that it be performed **BEFORE THE LORD.**

*And David danced **before the LORD** with all his might;... (2 Samuel 6:14)*

God's Word gives a number of reasons for dancing.

A. The Dance of Gratitude and Joy for Salvation

Dancing is a demonstration of gratitude for our salvation. When I say *salvation*, I do not just mean the initial salvation experience given to us by the Lord Jesus Christ. There is a countless list of obstacles, woes, calamities, tragedies and unseen circumstances that God spares us from and saves us from every day. The many ways that God saves us are innumerable. Therefore, let us not forget the many ways that He has saved us that we are not aware of.

Most Christians are familiar with the great story of Israel's deliverance from the bondage of Egypt and Egypt's ruler, Pharaoh. Egypt speaks to us of the world and Pharaoh speaks to us of the *self-life* or of the old carnal nature that holds us in bondage to the world. The old self is the false king that sits on the throne of our hearts and governs our life and brings us into bondage to the world. However, Jesus is the one true and real King that comes and delivers us from the bondage of the world, the self and the devil.

When Israel was under the bondage of this false king, God sent them a deliverer called Moses. He is a picture of our Redeemer, Jesus, who brings us out, and delivers from the house of bondage.

Israel was delivered from death by the blood of the slain lamb, which was placed over and down the sides of their doorposts. They walked out of Egypt that night and began their journey to the land of promise. Pharaoh and his army pursued them.

Just because you have the blood of salvation does not mean that your problems with the world are over. Pharaoh pursued Israel and desired to take them back into bondage.

Hence, God sent His people the cloud and the fire as a protection and comfort to them. (Exodus 13:21-22) The cloud and the fire are pictures of the Holy Ghost and fire which comforts us, leads us, and guides us, and is a wall of protection round about us. (John 14:17-18. 15:26-27, 16:13)

Then, God led the nation through the Red Sea by opening the waters and creating a dry path as Moses lifted up the rod over the sea. (Exodus 14:21-27, 1 Corinthians 10:2) When they reached the other side of the Red Sea, Pharaoh pursued after them. Moses lifted up the rod again and the false king and all of his army were buried in a watery grave. This is a picture of water baptism in the Name of the Lord Jesus Christ. (Acts 2:38, Romans 6:3, Galatians 3:27) The rod speaks of the Name of the Lord Jesus. It was the lifting up of the rod, or of the Name, that opened the sea. It is here in the waters of Jesus' Name, death and resurrection life that we see the old self buried in death. It is this "old former king" that wishes to drag us back to Egypt. We need the blood, fire and water experience daily to be wholly and completely separated from the world, the flesh and the devil.

What an experience it must have been for Israel to see their enemy and slave owners destroyed in the Red Sea. After Israel was safely on the other side, you can try to imagine the joy and the gratitude that flowed out of their hearts unto God.

And Miriam the prophetess, the sister of Aaron, took a timbrel in her hand; and all the women went out after her with timbrels and with dances. *And Miriam answered them, Sing ye to the LORD, for he hath triumphed gloriously: the horse and his rider hath he thrown into the sea. (Exodus 15:20-21)*

They danced before the LORD as a gratitude offering of joy and thanksgiving for their salvation.

We, too, have the privilege to lift our feet in gratitude to our Lord Jesus for the awesome experience of being set free from sin, from self and from the bondage of Egypt, the world. Oh, the gratitude that fills the heart when we realize that we were lost, but now we are found. If that alone does not place a desire within us to praise God in the dance then nothing ever will.

Another familiar story that shows us the gratitude dance for salvation is the story of the prodigal son. After having wasted all of his money, his inheritance from his father, the prodigal son finally came to his senses and decided to return to his father's house and plead for forgiveness. He returned home and said...

Father, I have sinned against heaven, and in thy sight, and am no more worthy to be called thy son. But the father said to his servants, Bring forth the best robe, and put it on him; and put a ring on his hand, and shoes on his feet: And bring hither the fatted calf, and kill it; and let us eat, and be merry: For this my son was dead, and is alive again; he was lost and is found. And they began to be merry. (Luke 15:21-24)

What a reception for the lost son! In the same manner God, the Father, treats His lost sheep that come home and find salvation and rest in Jesus. He also clothes us in righteousness, unites us to Himself, with a new ring of unity, strengthens our feet to walk in His ways, and feeds us. Oh, what joy we experience! The joy and the gratitude over the return and the salvation of the prodigal son caused great celebration, music and dancing in the father's house. Gratitude dancing was expressed on this incredible occasion.

The word for *dancing* in the above verse is *choros* in the Greek. It has exactly the same meaning as the Hebrew word *dances* from Exodus 15:20. These words both mean a *round dance* or, to dance in a circular motion. This circular dance is the dance of gratitude and joy for salvation.

Let us be diligent to demonstrate our joy and gratitude for deliverance and salvation with the dance!

Thou hast turned for me my mourning into dancing: thou hast put off my sackcloth, and girded me with gladness; To the end that my glory may sing praise to thee, and not be silent. O LORD my God, I will give thanks unto thee forever. (Psalm 30:11-12)

This is a powerful verse that I love very much. Here, we see mourning and heaviness turned into dancing while being girded with gladness (joy) and giving thanks unto the LORD (gratitude).

B. The Dance of Victory

The scriptures on dancing that have already been mentioned could also be used to express dances of victory. However, let's look at a particular place in God's Word where the victory dance was performed.

And it came to pass as they came, when David was returned from the slaughter of the Philistine (Gohath), that the women came out of all the cities of Israel, singing and dancing, to meet king Saul, with tabrets, with joy, and with instruments of music. And the women answered one another as they played, and said, Saul hath slain his thousands, and David his ten thousands. (1 Samuel 18:6-7)

The shepherd boy, David, brought a great victory to Israel the day that he slew the Philistine giant. The women came out dancing and playing music because of the victory that had been won.

There is something that I want to call to your attention in the verses above. Take note of what the women said as they danced their victory dance. They sang, *"Saul has slain his thousands and David has his slain ten thousands."*

Saul had already been king over Israel for some years when this episode with David and Goliath took place. He had won some battles with his army. Israel, under Saul, had slain their thousands. King Saul, therefore, received the honor that was due him.

Then this little guy David comes along and slays one man called Goliath and is given an honor which was ten times as great as the honor given King Saul. Was this deserved honor? Yes, indeed it was. The strength, or the cause for the Philistine's strength, lay in Goliath.

When David slew the root of the Philistine's strength, the army was dissolved and it became nothing.

Therefore, David ran and stood upon the Philistine, and took his sword, and drew it out of the sheath thereof, and slew him, and cut off his head therewith. ***AND WHEN THE PHILISTINES SAW THEIR CHAMPION WAS DEAD, THEY FLED.*** *(1 Samuel 17:51) (emphasis by author)*

In this illustration of scripture, we can learn a powerful principle that will benefit us greatly in our Christian walk.

When David slew Goliath, he dealt with the root of the matter. David managed to conquer the source of the Philistine army's strength and courage that was grounded in one man, Goliath. The many thousands of men that stood with Goliath were just little individual effects of one great cause. Within our lives, we have our problems that are, each and every one, the effect of a cause. In other words, every problem that we have has a root cause, whether it is spiritual, mental, emotional, physical or financial. Often times we are seemingly unable to overcome the Philistine army or all of the individual problems that we face. One of the reasons is because we are constantly struggling against all of the little individual effects, instead of dealing with the singular root cause. David went out and laid the axe to the root of the tree, as it were, and brought the life of the Philistine tree to naught.

We can have the same victory over our struggles and battles when we operate by the same principle. Ask God to reveal the root cause of your problems and then lay an axe to it.

And now also the axe is laid unto the root of the trees: therefore every tree which bringeth not forth good fruit is hewn down, and cast into the fire. (Matthew 3:10)

After you have put the axe to the root, get your feet moving in a victory dance over the destruction of *your Goliath.*

C. The Dance of The Marriage Union

Jesus Christ is going to marry a fully matured, spiritual bride who has her will joined in harmony and unity to His Will. His eyes seek and search for those who are prepared to say *"I do"* and who desire to enter into a oneness of relationship and fellowship with Him. Dancing unto the LORD is a prophetic demonstration that expresses the desire for such a union.

*And see, and, behold, if the daughters of Shiloh come out to **dance in dances,** then come ye out of the vineyards, and catch you every man his wife of the daughters of Shiloh, and* *go to the land of Benjamin... And the children of Benjamin did so, and took them wives, according to their number,* **of them that danced,** *whom they caught: and they went and returned unto their inheritance, and repaired the cities, and dwelt in them. (Judges 21:21,23)*

Shiloh was the location of the house, or Tabernacle of the LORD, for many years. The word Shiloh actually means an epithet (a descriptive word or phrase used in place of the usual name of a person) of the Messiah. Shiloh comes from the root word *Shalah* which means to be tranquil, serene or successful, to be happy, prosper and to be in safety.

Every year, the daughters of Shiloh made a pilgrimage to Shiloh to hold a feast unto the LORD in certain vineyards. This feast was held on the north side of Bethel. The name Bethel means house of God.

At the time that this story occurred, the Benjamites had been through a major tragedy. They had lost many of their women to war. The men of the tribe of Benjamin needed wives. The elders of the congregation of Israel counseled the men of Benjamin to go to Shiloh and to *take* for themselves wives. They were to choose only from the women that danced. The men did exactly what they were told to do.

The word "dance" from verse twenty-one in the scripture above is the Hebrew word *chawl.* This word means to twist or to whirl, to bear, to make to bring forth, to be in pain, to travail to birth with pain and to shake. It is a natural, as well as a spiritual fact, that there cannot be travail or a bringing forth of life until there has been a union of a male and a female.

The LORD wants His bride to come and hold a feast unto Himself at the place where his Name dwells. As we come and unite our wills to His will in marriage union, as it were, we can prophetically demonstrate that union and the bringing forth of new life by dancing. Through the prophetic dance, we attract the eyes of our precious bridegroom, Jesus Christ, who in turn will catch us away into new realms of a spiritual union, experience and fellowship with Himself.

When you desire a deeper and a greater relationship with your heavenly bridegroom, this great principle is a conduit or, a channel wherewith you can attract His holy eyes that search for willing hearts. You can prophetically demonstrate the fellowship that you desire with Jesus by dancing and believing that He will come and catch you up into a deeper oneness of relationship. The dancing also prophetically demonstrates the new life that is brought to birth through the bride and bridegroom relationship. Jesus, we desire a closer walk, a deeper fellowship, and a greater union with you. May we hold a feast unto the LORD and get caught away into His holy, and divine presence.

D. The Praise Dance

Let them praise his name in the dance... *(Psalm 149:3)*

The word praise in Hebrew is *halal*. This word means to be clear, to shine, to make a show and to boast. It also means to be clamorously foolish, to rave, to celebrate, to glory, to feign self-mad and to give in marriage.

In the second verse of Psalm 150, it tells us to praise God according to His excellent greatness. To praise God according to the amount of His greatness is an awesome amount of praise. The praise dance is a demonstration of God's greatness. People will only praise God according to how great they think He is. We will only praise Him to the level of our revelation of Him. The more that our eyes are opened to who He is, then the greater the show and the boasting of our God's greatness. We will, as a result, boisterously demonstrate His greatness in the praise dance.

King David is a classic example of one who praised God according to His excellent greatness. David danced before the LORD *with all of his might.*

And David danced before the LORD with all his might; and David was girded with a linen ephod.... And as the ark of the LORD came into the city of David, Michal Saul's daughter looked through a window, and saw David leaping and dancing before the LORD; and she despised him in her heart. (2 Samuel 6:14,16)

This particular incident took place when the Ark of the LORD was being brought to Zion to the tabernacle that David had prepared for it. The ark of God had been in the captivity of the Philistines. After the Philistines returned the ark to Israel, it remained for almost seventy years in the house of Abinadab. David had the vision of bringing the ark of God's presence back to God's people. He established a center of worship where the ark remained for forty years in the tabernacle that he had prepared for it. What a great day it was when God's presence and glory returned to the people of God.

David, clothed in the linen ephod of the high priest, praised God for the return of His presence in the midst of his people.

David did not just give a hop, a skip or a jump, rather he danced with every ounce of strength that he had within him. He demonstrated, or made a boastful show, of the greatness of the LORD God that dwelt between the cherubim. What a tremendous fulfillment of the commandment to love the LORD our God with all of our heart, all of our soul and all of our strength!

Even so, as David followed the ark and praised the LORD his God, Michal his wife, saw him and despised him in her heart. When David returned home to give a blessing to his household, he was met with a scornful, despising spirit from his wife.

Then David returned to bless his household. And Michal the daughter of Saul came out to meet David, and said, How glorious was the king of Israel today, who uncovered himself today in the eyes of the handmaids of his servants, as one of the vain fellows shamelessly uncovereth himself. (2 Samuel 6:20)

David was clothed in the linen undergarments of the high priest girded with the linen ephod. Michal looked upon David's behavior as an indecent humiliation for such a prominent person as he. To clarify, the linen undergarments of the priest were indeed decent, and covered David's whole body. Consequently, they were more modest and concealing than what many people wear in this age of nakedness.

And David said unto Michal, It was before the LORD, which chose me before thy father, and before all his house, to appoint me ruler over the people of the LORD, over Israel: therefore will I play before the LORD. And I will yet be more vile than thus, and will be base in mine own sight: and of the maidservants which thou hast spoken of, of them shall I be had in honour. (2 Samuel 6:21-22)

King David answered Michal's proud accusation by saying, in so many words, *"I did not dance before the maidservants to entertain them. My dancing was before the LORD."* He went on to say, in so many words, *"you think I was bad today, just wait a little, I intend to get worse. The greater my God becomes to me then the greater I will praise Him."* Verse twenty two begins by stating, *"I will be more vile than thus"*, This means, I plan on performing greater demonstrations of worship to my God as He becomes greater in my eyes and I become smaller in my own sight.

For her sin, Michal was punished with the severest possible punishment for an Oriental woman. As a result, she became barren.

Therefore Michal the daughter of Saul had no child unto the day of her death. (2 Samuel 6:23)

One of the reasons for the spiritual barrenness in the house of God today is due to the fact that many have despised the praises unto God and the liberty of the Spirit. So many have scorned and despised those who have demonstrated the greatness of their God in demonstrations of praise and worship. In spite, God wants to bring back the ark of His presence among His people. We need to, therefore, repent of our despising attitudes in order that we may be able to be free to demonstrate and hence, have our spiritual wombs opened so that they may bring forth life.

Chapter Five

STOMPING & TREADING
(Spiritual Warfare)

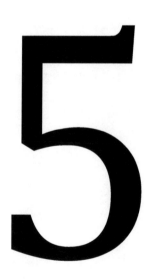

Let us remember that God wants to restore all things to His people. We have become extremely religious today in our churches that are full of traditions and forms. A tradition is simply something that has been done for so long that it has the force of law. Man made traditions that are allowed to govern the church will always create spiritual death.

In this generation, when the freedom and the liberty of the Spirit of God are mentioned, many will quote Paul's words to the Corinthians as an excuse to dismiss the move of the Spirit.

Let all things be done decently and in order. (1 Corinthians 14:40)

This verse has been used by many to cover up man's own pride and fear of being liberated in the Spirit and touched by God. To clarify, what *order* was Paul referring to? I do not believe for a moment that he was speaking of an order designed by man. He was referring to God's order! God's order is from the Word and the Spirit of God. Man's order is based on tradition. God's order is far superior to man's

71

order just as God's thoughts are superior to man's thoughts. *For as the heavens are higher than the earth, so are my ways higher than your ways, and my thoughts than your thoughts (Isaiah 55:9).*

Jesus was against the traditions and the rituals of man. He said...

But the hour cometh, and now is, when the true *worshippers shall worship the Father in spirit and in truth: for the Father seeketh such to worship him. God is a Spirit, and they that worship him must worship him in spirit and in truth. (John 4:23-24)*

It is high time that we learned to ascend above our carnal, fleshly feelings and seek God's order of worship. As long as we hold on to dead traditions and lifeless forms of religious practices, we will never be able to ascend into the heights of God's Spirit and Word. Let's examine what Jesus said concerning traditions in the following verses.

Then the Pharisees and scribes asked him, Why walk not thy disciples according to the tradition *of the elders, but eat bread with unwashen hands? He answered and said unto them, Well hath Isaiah prophesied of you hypocrites, as it is written, This people honoureth me with their lips, but their heart is far from me. Howbeit in vain do they worship me, teaching for doctrines the commandments of men. For laying aside the commandment of God, ye hold the tradition of men, as the washing of pots and cups: and many other such like things ye do. And he said unto them, Full well ye reject the commandment of God, that ye may keep your own tradition. (Mark 7:5-9)*

If I did not know any better, I would think that Jesus had been speaking directly to the religious scene of our day. The Pharisees, just like many church leaders in this generation, laid more importance and emphasis on fulfilling man's carnal tradition, which in their eyes was "decent and in order", rather than walking in obedience to the commandments of God.

Beware lest any man spoil you through philosophy and vain deceit, after the tradition of men, after the rudiments of the world, and not after Christ. (Colossians 2:8)

In this verse, God has given us a fourfold warning of what we are to be aware of in these last days lest we too become spoiled.

- Philosophy
- Vain Deceit
- Tradition of Men
- Rudiments of the World

1. Philosophy

The word philosophy means human knowledge or values. It means the general laws that furnish the rational explanation of anything. In other words, it is a particular set of ideas used to explain anything that was, is, or shall be.

There are many portions of scripture that cannot be explained or received by man's intellect. Rather, they are received by faith through the Spirit. It is such portions of scripture that cannot be explained by man's rationale, that have been rejected by many today. This is due to man's own inability to furnish a rational explanation that can appeal to the intellect.

Your walk with God starts and ends with faith. Salvation, on one side of the scales, cannot be explained or received by man's intellect. It is something that is quickened in man's spirit and has an effect on his deepest inner being, his heart. Beware of the philosophy of man's explanations that explain away simple but powerful truths in God's Word. It is of utmost importance to learn to walk in and accept the quickening of God's Word in your spirit by faith.

2. Vain Deceit

"Vain deceit" simply means thoughts that deceive the mind to think that something is worth the world when in truth it is worth nothing. It means fruitless, worthless and vanity.

How often have our minds been captured in vain deceit? We so easily let our minds get trapped into believing that the world and what it has to offer is of more value than the eternal things of God. There is not one Christian who has not been found in such a situation. Beware of vain deceit that comes your way. Put your affections on things above, or on that which has true meaning and eternal value.

3. Tradition

As already mentioned, a tradition is a custom that has been continued for so long that it has the force of law. This word also means doctrines and practices.

This is the very thing that kills the fire and life in the house of God today. So often, when God tries to move in a *new* way, or even in an *old* way, there are those who will boldly state, "Oh no, we can't have this or that in the church because we have never done things this way before." The religious world, the Christian world, the church, is stuck in many areas to the *way it has always been, or as we have always known it to be.* Hence, the way it has always been becomes a law to them. Beware of allowing the way you worship, or the way you pray, to become a form, or a law, or indeed a tradition.

4. Rudiments of the World

The word, *rudiments*, means conditions. It also means the orderly arrangement of this world. This has to do with lowering our standards to fit with the conditions and the order of this world. We do not have to become like the world to reach the world. We are in this world, but we are not of it. (John 17:14-16) Jesus never changed His way of walking, talking, living or communicating for the purpose of reaching the lost. Rather, He carried an anointing that broke the yokes. We do not need to be conformed to the image of the world to reach the world. On the contrary, the standards of God's will and purpose should be lifted up in our lives in all that we do and say. Walking, and living in the will of God produces an anointing that flows from our lives and sets captives free. Only the anointing breaks yokes. (Isaiah 10:27)

With these things in mind, let us examine what God's Word has to say concerning *stomping and treading* with regards to spiritual warfare. This is one of those demonstrative actions, used by the Spirit of God, which is hard for the carnal mind to grasp or to understand.

Which things also we speak, not in the words which man's wisdom teacheth, but which the Holy Ghost teacheth: comparing spiritual things with spiritual. But the natural man receiveth not the things of the Spirit of God: for they are foolishness unto him: neither can he know them, because they are spiritually discerned. (1 Corinthians 2:13-14)

Ask the Lord to open your spiritual eyes and ears that you may see and understand the precious mysteries concerning spiritual warfare.

Stomping and treading with the feet have basically to do with two things: destruction and warfare.

A. Destruction (Stomping)

Stomping is a visible demonstration of the destruction of false images and gods.

.. ,and he read in their ears all the words of the book of the covenant which was found in the house of the LORD. And the king stood by a pillar, and made a covenant before the LORD, to walk after the LORD, and to keep his commandments and his testimonies and his statutes with all their heart and all their soul, to perform the words of this covenant that were written in this book. And all the people stood to the covenant.... And he brought out the grove (image of a goddess) from the house of the LORD; and burned it at the brook Kidron, and stamped it small to

76

powder, and cast the powder thereof upon the graves of the children of the people. (2 Kings 23:2-3,6)

This scripture is referring to the days of King Josiah of Judah. The kings who had reigned before him had done that which was evil in the sight of the LORD. They had worshipped false gods and idolatrous images. But, King Josiah wanted to do that which was right in God's eyes.

During his reign, the book of the Law was found in the house of the LORD and was read before King Josiah. The fact that the book of the Law, the Torah, was *found* in the house of the LORD lets me know that it had been misplaced, ignored, or forgotten. Have we done the same thing today? Have the Word of God, His commands, and His desire for His house been misplaced, ignored, or forgotten?

Once the Law of God had been found and read, Josiah's desire was to rid the nation of all false gods and to encourage the people to serve the one true and living God. The idol images were removed from their high places, burned with fire, and *stomped* to total destruction, which rid the land of their presence.

Our bodies are the vessels or the temples of the Holy Ghost (1 Corinthians 6:19). God no longer dwells in buildings made by hands, but He makes His abode in the hearts of those who accept Him. God wants complete and total possession of these vessels as He does not want part ownership with idolatrous images and false gods.

Our temples, however, are full of false images. We have within us images of ourselves, we have false images of others, we have images of our careers, we have images of our possessions, we have images of our past and/or of our future, we have images of our purpose or ministries, and on and on we could go describing what our temples look like inside. We live to serve the images that we have created in the chambers of our imagery, deep within our own minds. (Ezekiel 8:12) Even so, God desires for us to permit the Holy Ghost fire to sanctify us from the bondage of these images and to burn them, as it were, to total ashes and stomp them to destruction under our feet. Jesus needs to be the one and only living image that has total possession of our temples.

Casting down *imaginations (thought, images), and every high thing that exalteth itself against the knowledge of God, and bringing into captivity every thought to the obedience of Christ; (2 Corinthians 10:5)*

The phrase *casting down* means to lower or with violence demolish, pull down, take down and destroy. Stomping is an outward visible demonstration of destroying, demolishing or casting down false images. As we go on for God and press deeper into the understanding of the corruption of our human hearts, the Word of God and the light of His Spirit will reveal all of the false images that possess portions of the temple of our hearts and of our minds. Let us be diligent to see these things in our lives and to pull them down, throw them out and to place them victoriously under our feet.

When Jesus went into the temple in Jerusalem, He cleaned it out. He did not enter the temple and accomplish His cleansing mission with some sweet talk or sugar cane. Rather, He went in with a scourge of small cords and *demonstrated* His holy anger against the falsehood that was taking place in the temple.

.And when he had made a scourge of small cords, he drove them all out of the temple, and the sheep, and the oxen; and poured out the changers' money, and overthrew the tables; And said unto them that sold doves, Take these things hence; make not my Father's house an house of merchandise. (John 2:13-17)

People ask the question, "Was Jesus angry?" The answer to that is: a resounding *yes, indeed yes!* He was demonstrating God's holy righteous anger against the corruption that was taking place in His Father's House of prayer.

God has given us the authority and the power of Jesus' almighty Name. We too can demonstrate the destruction and the putting down of the false images that are dwelling within our beings by stomping our feet in Holy Ghost demonstrations.

Through thee will we push down our enemies: through thy name will we tread them under that rise up against us. (Psalm 44:5)

The secret or power in stomping and treading under foot is in the Name of the Lord Jesus, the all-powerful Name above all other names. Without His Name (His power and authority) we can accomplish nothing.

79

Here a few more scriptures related to stomping.

Thus saith the Lord GOD; Smite with thine hand, and stamp with thy foot, and say, Alas for all the evil abominations of the house of Israel! for they shall fall by the sword, by the famine, and by the pestilence. (Ezekiel 6:ll)

And I took your sin, and calf which ye had made, and burnt it with fire, and stamped it, and ground it very small... (Deuteronomy 9:21)

... and Asa cut down her idol, and stamped it, and burnt it at the brook Kidron. (2 Chronicles 15:16)

B.   Warfare (Treading Under)

We now come to the other part in our study on the demonstrations of the feet where we will examine the topic of treading, or stomping in warfare.

Behold, I give unto you power to tread *on serpents and scorpions, and over all the power of the enemy: and nothing shall by any means hurt you. (Luke 10:19)*

Jesus is most definitely not talking about walking out into the middle of a jungle and deliberately finding serpents and scorpions to tread on so as to prove your spirituality and your powers. Even though I do believe that should something like that occur, we do possess the power in Jesus Name to walk away unharmed. (Acts 28:3-5) Even so, in the verse in Luke, chapter ten, Jesus was referring to spirits and to the power of spiritual foes. In verse twenty of that same chapter Jesus continued...

Notwithstanding in this rejoice not, that the spirits are subject unto you, but rather rejoice, because your names are written in heaven. (Luke 10:20)

It is clear and obvious that Jesus is definitely referring to spirits and demonic powers.

A serpent's bite and poison comes from its head, whereas a scorpion's poison comes from its tail.

Warfare

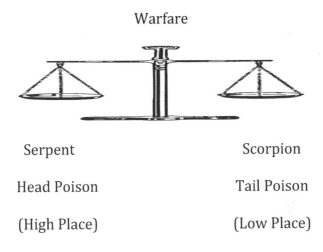

Serpent	Scorpion
Head Poison	Tail Poison
(High Place)	(Low Place)

This spiritual principle shows us that the enemy does not only attack us in the low place but also attacks us in the high place. Not only does he attack us frontally but also posteriorly, or from behind. No matter the position or spiritual location that we happen to be in when he attacks for the purpose of crippling our wills with his poison, we can put him under our feet with victorious demonstrations of treading under. With the all-powerful Name of Jesus and

His resurrected blood on our feet, we can war in the Spirit toward overcoming victory.

Thou shalt tread upon the lion and adder: the young lion and the dragon shalt thou trample under feet. (Psalm 91:13)

The lion, the adder and the dragon are titles that are used to picture our arch enemy, fallen Lucifer (1Peter 5:18, Revelation 20:2). Praise God for the victory of the cross! Jesus bruised the serpent's head and eternally put it under His feet when He won the battle over death, hell and the grave. Hallelujah!

And I will put enmity between thee and the woman, and between thy seed and her seed; it shall bruise thy head, and thou shalt bruise his heel. (Genesis 3:15)

The serpent, Lucifer, bruised the heel of Jesus when His feet were nailed to the cross. Yet, Jesus' blood stained heel bruised the head of the serpent crushing his power over humankind.

Chapter Six

JUMP & LEAPING

Have you ever won at a game of sports, or received some incredible news about someone or something, or maybe even been given the trip of a lifetime or a great gift? Often, our reaction to things like this is jumping, leaping or other expressions of joy. Joy cannot be contained. It is like an overflowing fountain gushing from the deep. Joy bubbles up like a spring of water that spurts out a life-giving river.

A. Joy

Jumping, leaping, and skipping are expressions and manifestations of joy. Upon the soul being touched by the hand of God, and when His powerful, fiery breath breathes upon the heart, it ignites a leaping in the feet for expressions of joyful praise.

And he leaping up stood, and walked, and entered with them into the temple, walking, and leaping, and praising God. (Acts 3:8)

Said with a loud voice, Stand upright on thy feet. And he leaped and walked. (Acts 14:10)

Oh the thrill, ecstasy and joy of being set free after having been bound in fetters that have prevented us from walking and moving forward. Jumping and leaping should be our expression of joy when God releases our feet, as it were, to walk with Him and to run the race that has been set before us. We have all been maimed by sin. We have all been crippled in our will. But, thank God for deliverance. Thank God for the ability to walk, to leap and to praise the Lord!

B. Overcoming

The word *leap* means to jump, to gush and to spring up. Jesus gave a powerful command to His disciples whom He knew would suffer great persecution for His Name's sake.

Blessed are ye, when men shall hate you, and when they shall separate you from their company, and shall reproach you, and cast out your name as evil, for the Son of man's sake. Rejoice ye in that day, and leap for joy: for, behold, your reward is great in heaven: for in the like manner did their fathers unto the prophets. (Luke 6:22-23)

Jumping, leaping and gushing forth with expressions of joy is usually the last thing that we consider doing when we are hated, when we have been separated from others, rejected, reproached, and when our names are dragged through the mud. Such attacks usually leave us feeling depressed and abandoned. However, Jesus knew the powerful effect of leaping for joy in such circumstances. Not only is leaping an expression of joy, but it also demonstrates overcoming. Leaping is an expression of getting over an obstacle that stands in your the way and is preventing you in your journey or in your success.

For by thee I have run through a troop; and by my God have I leaped over a wall. (Psalm 18:29)

Other's scorn and their rejection of us can be like an opposing troop and a wall of hindrance in our spiritual journey, calling or ministry. King David had a revelation of overcoming such obstacles. His revelation was to run and to leap. Is it any wonder the devil has fought so hard to snuff out the demonstrations of victorious overcoming such as dancing and leaping?

C. Revelation of The Word

I have often had a revelation in God's Word while studying, or while teaching, that has caused me to jump and to leap. The quickening power of Truth creates a fire within one's spirit that causes a "jump" in the feet.

The voice of my beloved! behold, he cometh leaping upon the mountains, skipping upon the hills. (Song of Songs 2:8)

The voice, or the Word, of the Beloved Bridegroom, Jesus, comes leaping and skipping upon the mountains and the hills of our souls and spirits. As He quickens His Word to us, the springs, fountains and wells of living water are released within our beings. How can one not jump and leap in joyful displays of quickening Truth?

When John the Baptist, not yet born, still in his mother Elizabeth's womb, heard the salutation of Mary, he leaped for joy.

And it came to pass, that, when Elisabeth heard the salutation of Mary, the babe leaped in her womb; and Elisabeth was filled with the Holy Ghost: For, lo, as soon as the voice of thy salutation sounded in mine ears, the babe leaped in my womb for joy. (Luke 1:41.44)

Mary was carrying the manifestation of the Living Word, in flesh, within her womb. As Mary spoke to Elizabeth about what had happened, her words reached the ears of John and created a leap for joy within him. This also happens to believers who hear the Word of God as He comes skipping into their hearts with quickening life and revelation.

The voice of God is full of quickening life. The quickened, revealed Word of God, causes the soul to soar to new heights. It causes the faint in heart to be strong. It causes the dry places to overflow with waters of life, and it causes a leaping and a jumping for joy within the weary soul.

The voice of the LORD breaketh the cedars; yea, the LORD breaketh the cedars of Lebanon. He maketh them also to skip like a calf; Lebanon and Sirion like a young unicorn. (Psalm 29:5-6)

The word used for "breaketh" is the Hebrew word *shaw-bar.* Among other things, this word means to *bring to birth.* King David referred to the cedars of Lebanon as the trees of the LORD. *"The trees of the Lord are full of sap; the cedars of Lebanon, which he hath planted;" (Psalm 104:16).* God likens us, His people, to trees that He has planted. (Isaiah 61:3). Just as the voice of the LORD caused His trees in Lebanon to skip like a calf, so His voice, His living Word, causes us to jump, to leap and to skip in joyful demonstrations of life!

Chapter Seven

SHAKING & TREMBLING

Shaking and trembling are both demonstrations that many people run a million miles from. I was guilty of doing the very same thing in my own ignorance. Most of my experience with shaking and trembling had been with people who violently trembled while demons were being cast out of them and when the evil spirits were manifesting themselves. It is true that evil spirits do manifest themselves in this manner. Regardless, let us also remember that all of the devil's tactics and ways were stolen from God. If there is ever a day when we need discernment to know the difference between the moving of God's Spirit and the manifestation of demons it is most definitely today. We must be careful not to throw away God's blessing of restoration due to our own lack of discernment or because of our own ignorance. However, we must also be careful not to be overtaken by spirits that reveal themselves as angels of light and are sent to lead the church astray. (Galatians 2:4; 2 Peter 2:1-2)

I have had the privilege of ministering in churches in fifty-eight countries and on six continents. As a result, I have seen and experienced many things. One of the saddest things that I have witnessed, however, is the lack of knowledge in God's Word accompanied by the lack of spiritual discernment that the leaders of many churches possess.

On one of my many trips to Asia, I was ministering in a church one night where the presence and the power of God moved in an extra ordinarily powerful way. People were being saved, healed, and delivered. One sister whom I prayed for began shaking from head to toe. The pastor and a few other ministers were immediately on the scene and began to rebuke the devil and to command the evil spirits to come out of her. The only problem was that this sister was not demon possessed. The power of God had, however, overwhelmed her mightily. I asked my brothers to stop rebuking and to start praising God with her. They did not understand, but they did what I asked anyway. After a few moments, one of the ministers had the same experience as the sister. He too began shaking and trembling and fell prostrate whilst praise in the Spirit rolled from his mouth. This continued to happen until the fire of this liberating, cleansing experience engulfed the auditorium. It was an amazing sight to behold as God's people experienced an earthquake that opened their tombs of spiritual death, as it were. As was evidenced by this example, we need discernment and understanding in the realms of the spirit.

I acknowledge and am fully aware that demonic forces do manifest themselves with shaking and with other physical demonstrative actions. This study, however, is solely dealing with the demonstration of shaking and trembling under the power, guidance, and the influence of the Holy Ghost.

A.   Breaking Free From Bondage

Shaking under the power of God has an overwhelming influence on one's body, soul, spirit and will. As already stated in this book, the things in the natural realms relate to those things in the spiritual realms. In the natural, when we get caught in a spider's web, or a creature fastens itself or it clings to us, what do we do? We shake ourselves free. It is an automatic response.

Awake, awake; put on thy strength, O Zion; put on thy beautiful garments, O Jerusalem, the holy city: for hence forth there shall no more come into thee the uncircumcised and the unclean. Shake thyself from the dust; arise, and sit down, O Jerusalem: loose thyself from the bands of thy neck, O captive daughter of Zion. (Isaiah 52:1-2)

In this passage of scripture the LORD is speaking to His bride, Jerusalem. The message was for her to awaken and to be clothed with the beautiful garments of praise, salvation and righteousness. (Isaiah 61:3.10) She was to shake herself free from the dust and to be loosed from the bondage around her neck (the neck speaks of the will). The meanings of the words of this scripture in Hebrew reveal to us a deeper understanding of what God was saying. The word dust in Hebrew is *aphar* and it means clay, earth, mud, ashes, ground, mortar, powder and rubbish. The Bible teaches us that dust, clay, and ashes are pictures of the world and of the flesh. (Genesis 2:7) The dust of the world relates to the lust of the flesh, the lust of the eyes, and the pride of life among the many other things of the world that bind us.

For all that is in the world, the lust of the flesh, and the lust of the eyes, and the pride of life, is not of the Father, but is of the world. (1 John 2:16)

The word for shake in Hebrew is *na'ar*. This word means the rustling of the mane, which usually accompanies the lion's roar. It means to tumble about, shake off, shake self, overthrow and toss up and down. *Na'ar* also means to growl and yell. The LORD was beckoning His bride to arise and free herself from the influence and from the bondage of the world by shaking the dust off of her. The *shaking* was to be accompanied by the roar of the Lion of the tribe of Judah. This roar, along with this shaking was, and is, endued with overcoming power when the Holy Ghost lightens upon it. It is the Lion of the tribe of Judah who has prevailed. His *roar* is powerful! (Revelation 5:5)

Jesus gave a similar charge to His disciples.

And whosoever shall not receive you, nor hear your words, when ye depart out of that house or city, shake off the dust of your feet. (Matthew 10:14)

The word *shake* in this verse in Greek is *tinasso*. It means to swing, to shake violently and to shake off. Jesus cautioned His disciples not to let the dust of rejection stick to their feet from the places where the Word of God was rejected. Do not let the dust of other people's rebellious attitudes affect your own walk with God. Shake it off and be free from those binding spirits. It is so easy to allow the spirit of rejection of this world to impact our choices and our walk with God. Thus, when you feel that your feet are beginning to walk in the wrong direction and maybe taking you in the opposite direction of God's purpose, shake the sinful, heavy dust off of yourself and continue to walk in the freedom of the Spirit of God.

The world, the flesh and the devil try so desperately to bind us in chains. The following verses speak of Paul and Silas.

And when they had laid many stripes upon them, they cast them into prison, charging the jailor to keep them safely: Who, having received such a charge, thrust them into the inner prison, and made their feet fast in the stocks. (Acts 16:23-24)

We may never experience this sort of bondage naturally speaking, but we have all most certainly experienced this in a spiritual sense. The world, the flesh and the devil work well as a team of jailors in order to keep our feet fastened and bound in stocks, as it were, so as to prevent us in our walk with, and service to God. Notwithstanding, God uses certain ways and methods to release us out of these bondages.

And at midnight Paul and Silas prayed, and sang praises unto God: and the prisoners heard them. And suddenly there was a great earthquake so that the foundations of the prison were shaken: and immediately all the doors were opened and every one's bands were loosed. (Acts 16:25-26)

As the praises belched out of Paul and Silas unto God, something began to happen. Everyone heard them as they sang out their sacrificial praises. Suddenly, God's power began to move. An earthquake materialized and shook the very foundation of Paul and Silas' bondage. Everything began to shake. The stocks about their feet were released. The chains about them fell off. The prison doors were opened and everyone was set free.

God has not changed His way of doing things. He is still the same powerful liberating God! In Paul and Silas' case, God did not have to shake everything as He did to set them free. He could have just lifted them up and brought them out with His miracle working hand. However, God operates by principles and according to His own divine Laws. In this particular incident, God demonstrated the liberating power of *shaking*. Shaking with an earthquake!

This can, and will work for us as well. When in bondage, if we will only but begin to shout and offer praises to the Name of the LORD, God will cause His power to shake the very foundation of whatever it is that holds us in bondage. The greatest thing about all of this is that it is real and it works. A good shaking under the anointing of God's Spirit will indeed break bondages and liberate you!

The liberating power that sets us free is a product of what Jesus accomplished on Calvary.

Jesus, when he had cried again with a loud voice, yielded up the ghost. And, behold, the veil of the temple was rent in twain from the top to the bottom; and the earth did quake, (to rock, vibrate, tremble, move, shake) and the rocks rent; And the graves were opened; and many bodies of the saints which slept arose. (Matthew 27:50-52)

When Jesus' work on the cross was accomplished, a powerful thing took place. The ground that held the bodies of the overcoming Old Testament saints began to shake. The rocks rent and the earth yielded the bodies of those held captive. This is the true effect of the cross of Calvary. The work Jesus accomplished on the cross will bring us up out of death, bondage and despair. If the son, therefore, shall make you free, ye shall be free indeed. (John 8:36)

Many in the church today are guilty of making the cross of *none effect*. This was not so with the Apostle Paul.

For Christ sent me not to baptize, but to preach the gospel: not with wisdom of words, lest the cross of Christ should be made of none effect. For the preaching of the cross is to them that perish foolishness; but unto us which are saved it is the power of God. (1 Corinthians 1:17-18)

The cross becomes of no or of none effect when it is dressed up with man's carnal wisdom. People cover it with make-up and jewelry, so to speak, and make it look all flowery and pleasant. The cross is dressed up to appeal to the masses, hiding its true identity as the place of shame, suffering and pain. The cross of Christ was a humiliating death experience. Walking the way of the cross is also a humiliating death experience. Taking up our cross daily is a humiliating death experience. Taking up our cross means death to self. The cross means absolute abandonment of one's own preferences, one's own will and one's own desires in favor of His, the Lord Jesus. Walking the way of the cross means mortification of everything within me that contraries everything that is God.

However, after death comes the resurrection and life. We need to look back to Calvary with the prophetic eyes of the Spirit of God and see the bloody, humiliating scene of death for what it really was. Then, the cross will accomplish its full effect and purpose in our lives.

The effect of the cross generates tremendous power. As a matter of fact, all overcoming power is generated through the cross of Calvary. I have often likened the cross to electrical wires. A lamp, for example, has a cord connected to it with a plug at the end of the wire. When plugged into an electrical power outlet the flow of electricity through the cord will cause the bulb to light up. The evidence of power moving through the cord is clearly seen in the light. In any case, you cannot feel the power that creates the light because the wires are covered with insulation. Yet, if the wires were to be stripped of the covering insulation then the power generated through the wires would no doubt shake or jolt you if you were to touch them. Ever had such an experience? I have and it gave me quite a jolt.

The cross operates the same way. There are many who see the powerful effect of the cross, but they do not experience it for themselves. Calvary becomes of no effect to many because it is dressed up, or covered with the insulation of man's reasoning and carnal wisdom. But, when we strip the cross down to what it really is and lay ahold of the humility of Calvary, then the generating power of the cross will flow through you and it will set you free. Praise God!

Jesus, Himself, was delivered out of the tomb of death through a shaking earthquake.

And behold, there was a great earthquake; for the angel of the Lord descended from heaven, and came and rolled back the stone from the door, and sat on it. (Matthew 28:2)

Praise God for the liberating, powerful effect of Calvary!

B. Warfare

Shaking, in the scriptures, also has to do with warfare, destruction and judgment.

Deliver thyself, O Zion, that dwellest with the daughter of Babylon. For thus saith the LORD of hosts; After the glory hath he sent me unto the nations which spoiled you: for he that toucheth you toucheth the apple of his eye. For, behold, I will shake mind hand upon them, and they shall know that the LORD of hosts hath sent me. (Zechariah 2:7-9)

Israel was in bondage and captivity to Babylon. God made a demonstration of war and destruction against Babylon by the shaking of His hands.

I can remember when I was a child standing next to a dear old saint of God during a church service. As we praised the Lord and the power and the presence of God began to flow, the sister's hands began to shake. Even as a child, I knew that there was something special about it. It always attracted my attention, but I did not understand this powerful demonstration until much later in life.

How awesome it has been to grow up and to find the answers in God's Word. The shaking of the hands is a true demonstration of war and destruction.

Blessed be the LORD my strength, which teacheth my hands to war, and my fingers to fight: (Psalm 144:1)

In that day shall Egypt be like unto women: and it shall be afraid and fear because of the shaking of the hand of the LORD of hosts, which he shaketh over it.(Isaiah 19:16)

When the hands of the LORD begin to shake, and as He moves His people to demonstrate with this act of war, and we join ourselves to His hands, so to speak, the enemy becomes feeble and fearful and will flee. God wants to remove all hindrances and obstacles of the enemy in order that we may walk on a cleared pathway.

And the LORD shall utterly destroy the tongue of the Egyptian sea; and with his mighty wind shall he shake his hand over the river, and smite it in the seven streams, and make men go over dryshod. (Isaiah 11:15)

This verse is a prophecy concerning the restoration of Israel and the return of the remnant and the outcasts of Israel and Judah to their own land. In order for their return to be fully accomplished, an obstacle, or an enemy had to be removed. In this particular case, it was the Egyptian sea. The LORD promised to shake His hand over the problem and to create a *dryshod* pathway for men to walk on. God has not changed! He still does the same for us today as we trust in Him and as we walk with Him.

C. God's Presence

Standing in the awesome presence of God causes mankind to shake and to quiver with a fearful respect for God's righteousness, holiness and for His almighty Word, or voice.

Tremble thou earth, at the presence of the LORD, at the presence of the God of Jacob. (Psalm 114:7)

There is a definite lack of fear and respect towards the Lord within the church today. This, however, is not only true within the church. People disrespect each other in general. One can clearly see displays of disrespect among the general public many times a day. Husbands are disrespectful to their wives, and wives likewise, are disrespectful to their husbands. Children are disobedient and disrespectful to their parents and also toward other figures of authority. There is a lack of respect for law enforcement officers as well as for schoolteachers. Likewise, the church is disrespectful toward leaders. All of this disrespect that is evident in the world today stems from one root problem and that said problem is a lack of respect for God and for His laws of life. Still, God wants us to fear and tremble in His presence and at His Word. This means that He desires for His people to have a fearful respect and an honor towards Him and towards His will. As a result this causes us to respect all other forms of life.

Hear the word of the LORD, ye that tremble at his word;...(Isaiah 66:5)

Habakkuk also trembled at the word and the majesty of God.

When I heard, my belly trembled; my lips quivered at the voice: rottenness entered into my bones, and I trembled in myself, that I might rest in the day of trouble: when he cometh up unto the people, he will invade them with his troops. (Habakkuk 3:16)

Moses trembled in the presence of the LORD as God spoke and revealed Himself to him.

And when forty years were expired, there appeared unto him in the wilderness of Mount Sina an angel of the Lord in a flame of fire in a bush. When Moses saw it, he wondered at the sight: and as he drew near to behold it, the voice of the Lord came unto him, Saying, I am the God of thy father, the God of Abraham, and the God of Isaac, and the God of Jacob. Then Moses trembled, and durst not behold. (Acts 7:30-32)

When the Lord called Saul on his way to Damascus, Saul, with a trembling respect, asked God what He would have him to do.

And as he journeyed, he came near Damascus: and suddenly there shined round about him a light from heaven: And he fell to the earth, and heard a voice saying unto him, Saul, Saul, why persecutest thou me? And he said, Who art thou, Lord? And the Lord said, I am Jesus whom thou persecutest: it is hard for thee to kick against the pricks.

And he trembling and astonished said, Lord, what wilt thou have me to do? And the Lord said unto him, Arise, and go into the city, and it shall be told thee what thou must do. (Acts 9:3-6)

We need this fear of God that will cause us to take heed to the Word of the Lord and to humble ourselves in obedience to His authority and headship. Do not be afraid to demonstrate that respect to the LORD and His Word if the Spirit of God should fall upon you with shaking and trembling while you bask in His awesome presence. God desires this of those who serve Him.

Daniel 6:26; Isaiah 64:2; 1 Corinthians 2:3

Here are a few more scripture references concerning the fear of the LORD:

Proverbs 2:l-5; Proverbs1:28-29; Proverbs 8:13; Proverbs 9:10; Proverbs 10:27; Proverbs 14:27; Proverbs 19:23.

Chapter Eight

NOISE & SHOUT

Once again, we are looking at a subject that has much to do with the law of balance. Of course, there is no balance without opposites. We would not have electricity, for example, without this universal law of positive and negative. So, it is with the noise and the shout. The opposite of these is the quiet (silence) and the whisper.

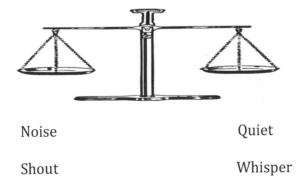

Noise	Quiet
Shout	Whisper

As already mentioned, God is a God of perfect balance. He is a God that loves noise and a God that loves silence. We will take a look at silence in the following chapter.

Make a joyful noise unto the LORD, all the earth: make a loud noise, *and rejoice, and sing praise. (Psalm 98:4)*

O come, let us sing unto the LORD: let us make a joyful noise to the rock of our salvation. Let us come before his presence with thanksgiving, and make a joyful noise unto him with psalms. (Psalm 95:1-2)

Sing aloud unto God our strength: make a joyful noise unto the God of Jacob. (Ps 81:1)

It is obvious from these verses, plus many more, that God loves the loud joyful noise and the sound of praises. Human beings are great artists in crossing and unbalancing God's scales. What God calls sweet man calls bitter. What God calls death man calls life. Light is darkness and darkness is light to the fallen view of humankind. Likewise, we also have the tendency to rearrange and unbalance the scales of noise and silence.

Christianity has become divided between these two opposites. Some are so still and quiet in their churches that you can hear a pin drop. Others are so noisy and loud in their music and song that one can barely hear one's own thoughts, let alone the thoughts of God. The noisy extremists focus on producing noise, and lots of it, in their services. They judge the outcome of their services according to how much noise and demonstrative action was present in their service. On the other hand, the quiet extremists judge the outcome of their services by the stillness and so-called reverence and peace that they have experienced in their time with the Lord. They are firm believers that the more people fall asleep in their pews the greater the peace in their midst. The *"quietness people"* rebuke all noise and even consider it to be of the devil.

God wants balance in the church. Noise is necessary but so is stillness and quietness before the Lord. We must learn to let the Holy Ghost have his way in our midst and not attempt to try to dominate or govern our services with a program or a personal preference. If the joyful noise, shouts of praise, music and boisterous demonstrations were not a necessity then God would not have wasted the time to instruct us in His Word concerning these things.

I have been to countries where the nationals are of the opinion that noise and demonstrative worship in the church is acceptable in some countries and cultures but definitely not in their own country. They believe that their culture is different and that God never intended for them to make a noise in church or in active worship to Him. Culture or no culture, God has given one Bible to all nations. Whether you are black, white, yellow, red or brown, when we enter the presence of God there is only one authority and that is His!

There is nothing at all wrong with culture as long as the culture does not oppose the Word of God. In God's house and in His presence, the culture of His Word and the move of His Spirit rules. If our culture is contrary to His Will we need to lay the culture down. God gave one book of rules, the Bible, for all people of all nations.

Make a joyful noise unto God, ***all ye lands***. *(Psalm 66:1)*

In 1983, I had the privilege of ministering in a Scandinavian country. The locals strictly resisted the move of the Holy Ghost and claimed that they were different from other nations. They earnestly and sincerely believed that God did not expect them to yield to the move of His Spirit as He did other nations. They informed me that, as a nation, the people were reserved, quiet and certainly not the loud outspoken or demonstrative type.

A few days after my ears had been bombarded with these and many more excuses, I was invited to the home of the pastor for dinner. It was the annual national holiday and was a day of great celebration. All sorts of activities were going on in honor of celebrating the most festive day of the year.

We had just finished enjoying a delightful afternoon coffee served with national delicacies when all of a sudden, from the distance, I heard a tremendous roar of unified shouts and screams coming from the harbor that was located about a mile or so away. We opened the window to listen and observe what the commotion may have been all about. We saw and heard hundreds of people jumping, clapping and shouting at the top of their voices. There was a thunderous roar of human voices. People were cheering and whistling as the national rowing clubs were competing within the inner harbor. Immediately, I gave the remark that all of those people cheering and *carrying on* must be foreigners. Oh no, I was told that they were locals cheering for their favorite rowing teams. Guess what! They acted like any other nation would act at a rowing competition, a football match, a baseball game, or any other sports event.

Later that day we took a walk down town to enjoy the activities, singing and presentations taking place. Many were intoxicated with wine and beer and strangely enough they also acted exactly the same as intoxicated people act all around the world.

I liken what I saw that day to the spiritual. It does not matter what culture or background you come from. When you get excited about the LORD and His Word and become intoxicated (filled) with the new wine of His Spirit then your culture goes out the window and you begin to act exactly the same way that all of the rest of God's people act under the power and the influence of His Spirit. The problem with these people was not their culture but their pride. Pride will choke and destroy any form of life that God wants to bring to birth in you. So, let us give a good shout for the LORD our God who reigns in all nations!

Reasons for Noise and Shouts of Praise

A. Joy

It is a natural response in human beings to make a noise when the emotions are bubbling with joy. God wants us to express our joy, thrill and excitement of knowing Him and walking with Him. We can express our love and gratitude by rejoicing with shouts of praise.

But let all those that put their trust in thee rejoice: let them ever shout for joy, because thou defendest them: let them also that love thy name be joyful in thee. *(Psalm 5:11)*

Let thy priests be clothed with righteousness; and let thy saints shout for joy. *(Psalm 132:9)*

I will also clothe her priests with salvation: and her saints shall shout aloud for joy. *(Psalm 132:16)*

The people of God are the only ones upon the face of the earth that have anything worth shouting about. The world shouts over sports, music, accomplishments, and for their great stars and idols. The victories of this world come and go, as do the stars and the idols that humans adore. But, Jesus is the bright and the morning star and He will shine throughout eternity. The victory that He has won over death and His opponent is permanent and eternal. Now that's something to really shout about!

Sing, O daughter of Zion; shout, O Israel; be glad and rejoice with all the heart, O daughter of Jerusalem. The LORD hath taken away thy judgments, he hath cast out thine enemy: the king of Israel, even the LORD, is in the midst of thee: thou shalt not see evil any more. In that day it shall be said to Jerusalem, Fear thou not: and to Zion, Let not thine hands be slack. The LORD thy God in the midst of thee is mighty; he will save, he will rejoice over thee with joy; he will rest in his love, he will joy over thee with singing, (Zephaniah 3:14-17)

Beloved, be diligent to rejoice and to shout over the victory of your salvation. Praise God in demonstrations of joyful sound because our God has removed the judgments against us.

Psalm 32:11; Psalm 35:37; Psalm 65:3; Psalm 132:9-16

B. War and Triumph

O clap your hands, all ye people; shout unto God with the voice of triumph. (Psalm 47:1)

We have already mentioned that the victory that Jesus has won is an eternal everlasting triumph. He can never be defeated. His victory is permanent and perpetual. Because Jesus has won the victory, we can go into battle against the enemy of our souls with the shout of triumphant praise. We are the beneficiaries of the accomplished triumph and the victory won on the cross of Calvary.

Israel won many battles with the shouts of triumphant praise to God. One such battle was the famous battle and victory at Jericho.

Israel finally entered Canaan's land after a forty-year journey of wandering in the wilderness. After they entered the land, God's plan for Israel was to go and to possess, and to occupy their promised inheritance. The city of Jericho was Israel's first battle and their first victory in Canaan.

And ye shall compass the city, all ye men of war, and go round about the city once. Thus shalt thou do six days. And seven priests shall bear before the ark seven trumpets of rams horns: and the seventh day ye shall compass the city seven times, and the priests shall blow with the trumpets. And it shall come to pass, that when they make a long blast with the ram's horn, and when ye hear the sound of the trumpet, all the people shall shout with a great shout; and the wall of the city shall fall down flat, and the people shall ascend up every man straight before him. (Joshua 6:3-5)

God commanded Joshua to gather the men of war and to walk around the city of Jericho for six days, once per day. Then, on the seventh day they were to walk around the city seven times. This makes a total of thirteen times that they marched around the city walls. Six is the number of man and seven is the number of completion and of the Son of God. When man joins his will in *marriage union,* as it were, to the will of the perfect one, Jesus Christ, then victory in claiming our spiritual inheritance is the result. Six plus seven equals thirteen. For many the number thirteen is an evil or unlucky number. But just like everything else that the devil has stolen the number thirteen carries the revelation of the Bride and Bridegroom relationship.

Israel had entered into Canaan, or Beulah land. As they entered the land of promise, God brought them into a binding *marriage* covenant with Himself.

Thou shalt no more be termed Forsaken; neither shall thy land any more be termed Desolate: but thou shalt be called Hephzibah, and thy land Beulah: for the LORD delighteth in thee, and thy land shall be married. (Isaiah 62:4)

Beulah means to marry a husband, to be a wife, and to enter into marriage. The promised inheritance was that of union, fellowship and relationship with the God of Israel. This too is the ultimate spiritual destiny for us as spiritual Israel.

Seven priests walked before the Ark of the Covenant that day as they marched around the walls of Jericho. They carried seven trumpets of rams' horns. The ark speaks of God's Kingship and ruler-ship. It represents His throne, His presence, His glory and His Law. The seven ram's horns speak of the complete power of God. Horns always depict power and strength. One may ask, "Was the blowing of the horns not enough for Israel to get the victory over Jericho?" "Was the display of God's power and strength in the ram's horns not sufficient to take the walls down?" The answer is a resounding, "Obviously not!" After the thirteenth trip around the walls the priests were commanded to blow the trumpets and all of the people were commanded to shout with a great shout. There is a divine principle is involved here.

There are two Hebrew words used for shout in Joshua chapter six verse five. The first word is *ruwa* which means to split the ears with sound, shout for alarm or joy, blow an alarm and cry aloud. It means to destroy, make a joyful noise and triumph. (Strongs #7321)

The second word for shout is *truwak* This word means a battle cry, clamour, jubilee, loud noise. (Strongs #8643)

God commanded Israel to unite their voices with a loud, joyful, triumphant battle cry to the sound of the seven trumpets. Here, we see the union of the divine power of God and the voices of His people ringing out in one sound of triumphant victory over the enemy. As Israel united to the will of God and performed what He had commanded, victory was the result in their battles and new territory was gained.

This principle of Truth still works. I have seen many victories take place before my eyes as God's people have united their voices with the power and the anointing of the Holy Ghost. In unity have shouted a victorious battle cry that defeated the enemy and the powers of darkness.

Shouts of anointed praise and battles cries pierce the darkness of the spiritual wickedness in high places.

So the people shouted when the priests blew with the trumpets: and it came to pass, when the people heard the sound of the trumpet, and the people shouted with a great shout, that the wall fell down flat, so that the people went up into the city, every man straight before him, and they took the city. (Joshua 6:20)

Another great example of the noise of the battle shout/cry and the trumpet, is in the story of the battle between Abijah, king of Judah, and Jeroboam, king of Israel.

At this particular time, Israel had departed from the ways of the LORD, but Judah had not. Judah had remained faithful to the LORD their God. King Abijah of Judah rose up to speak against the rebellion and the wickedness of Israel in hope that Israel might repent and return to God. King Jeroboam of Israel, obviously, did not like what he heard. He sent 800,000 men to war against Judah. He planted an ambush against Judah that surrounded their armies both from before and from behind.

And when Judah looked back, behold, the battle was before and behind: and they cried unto the LORD, and the priests sounded with the trumpets. Then the men of Judah gave a shout: and as the men of Judah shouted, it came to pass, that God smote Jeroboam and all Israel before Abijah and Judah. And the children of Israel fled before Judah: and God delivered them into their hand. (2 Chronicles 13:14-16)

As the trumpets of God's power sounded, the people shouted with the voice of triumph and a battle cry. In an instant, God smote the armies of Israel and they fled. There is tremendous power in the shouts of victory when the saints of God shout under the anointing of the Spirit of God.

Our opponent, the dragon, called the old devil, serpent, and Satan, along with all of his armies, tremble as God's people shout the almighty Name that has overcome them. There is tremendous authority and power in shouting the Name of the Lord Jesus in a triumphant battle cry against the principalities, the powers, the rulers of the darkness of this world and the spiritual wickedness in high places. (Revelation 12:9; Ephesians 6:12)

... the devils also believe, and tremble. (James 2:19)

We have more than enough reason to shout because of our triumphant King Jesus!

Zechariah prophesied concerning Jesus, the great king, who brought His people justice and salvation:

Rejoice greatly, O daughter of Zion; shout, O daughter of Jerusalem: behold, thy King cometh unto thee: he is just, and having salvation; lowly, and riding upon an ass, and upon a colt the foal of an ass. (Zechariah 9:9)

This was the prophecy of Jesus' triumphant entry into Jerusalem. Matthew recorded this victorious day in his gospel, chapter twenty-one. As the multitudes shouted, "Hosanna to the son of David," the religious people of the day tried to silence the crowd. Nothing has changed from then until now. Religion has all but killed the move of the Spirit of God. Religion has silenced true worship. The religious people are the ones that disliked the triumphant shout to the son of David in the days of Jesus. Unfortunately, we face the same opposition today. Forget your religion and religious practices and grasp hold of a true relationship with the son of David, Jesus Christ. Shout to the Lord!

The response that Jesus gave to the Pharisees rebuke was priceless.

He answered and said unto them, I tell you that, if these should hold their peace, the stones would immediately cry out. (Luke 19:40)

I believe with all of my heart that one of the reasons that nature is going wild in these last days is due to God's people who have failed to honor the God of creation with triumphant praises. Nature is crying out more than ever through earthquakes, winds, floods, fires, volcanoes, storms and the like. Never in recent history have there been so many natural disasters recorded as in the past fifty years. Can this be because God's people have failed to cry out and shout to the God of the universes? God not only wants, but He commands His people to shout and demonstrate His awesome power and presence. So, let's get together and make a noise of eternal victory unto our God. He is worthy!

C. Cleansing

The demonstration of noise and of shouting also has to do with cleansing.

And his feet like unto fine brass, as if they burned in a furnace; and his voice as the sound of many waters. (Revelation 1:15)

Why did Jesus appear to John the Apostle with the Word coming out of His mouth with a sound greater than Niagara Falls? The beginning of John's revelation was concerning the seven churches in Asia Minor. The seven churches were prophetic pictures of the seven church ages to come.

Each one of the seven churches had obstacles to overcome. Each church, and church age to follow, needed cleansing. Jesus had a word for each church. Not only did He have a word of encouragement, but He also had a word of rebuke and of cleansing. His Word came out like a mighty waterspout to wash away and to cleanse the defilement just like one would use a water hose to clean a pathway. The more pressure that is sprayed out of the nozzle; the cleaner the pathway will be. God wants His people to be clean and shining with the glory of His holiness.

And, behold, the glory of the God of Israel came from the way of the east: and his voice was like the noise of many waters: and the earth shined with his glory. (Ezekiel43:2)

The voice of the LORD comes with a great noise like a mighty rushing, cleansing stream of water. We can prophetically demonstrate the pouring forth of God's Word like mighty waters through the demonstrations of the lifting of our voices. The noise and the shout create a pathway for the Word of God to flow and to minister it's life and cleansing power to us.

Hear attentively the noise of his voice, and the sound that goeth out of his mouth. (Job 37:2)

D. Praise

Noise and shouting are also demonstrations of praise and worship to the LORD.

And they sang together by course in praising and giving thanks unto the LORD; because he is good, for his mercy endureth for ever toward Israel. And all the people shouted with a great shout, when they praised the LORD, because the foundation of the house of the LORD was laid But many of the priests and Levites and chief of the fathers, who were ancient men, that had seen the first house, when the foundation of this house was laid before their eyes, wept with a loud voice; and many shouted aloud for joy: So that the people could not discern the noise of the shout of joy from the noise of the weeping of the people: for the people shouted with a loud shout, and the noise was heard afar off. (Ezra 3:11-13)

These verses are referring to the rebuilding of the temple in Jerusalem, after Israel's return from exile and captivity in Babylon. On this occasion, the people gathered together to celebrate the completion of the foundation of the temple. Take note, no walls were yet built. There was no roof, no pillars, and no structure, only the foundation had been laid. The people shouted in praise to God for the foundation.

Often, people have to wait for the completion of God's blueprints and master plans in their lives before they can shout out in praise and honor to God. We want to see, or experience, a complete and finished "building" before we give God the honor that is due to His Name.

We were given an example for our benefit of how Israel praised God when only the foundation had been completed. We, too, should practice the same level of faith and worship and believe that He who has begun a good work in us will perform and complete what He started. (Philippians 1:6)

God is gone up *with a* shout, *the LORD with the sound of a trumpet. Sing praises to God, sing praises: sing praises unto our King, sing praises. (Psalm 47:5-6)*

Chapter Nine

SILENCE

Silence demonstrates a particular move of God's Spirit just as much as noise does. As already mentioned in the previous chapter, it is important that we be led by God's Spirit to find the balance between the noise and the silence in His presence. Some despise the noise while others despise the quietness, but God wants us to experience both. Both of these opposite sides to the character of God and the revelation of Himself have great spiritual significance.

... a time to keep silence... (Ecclesiastes 3:7)

There is a time for silence. The word silence in Hebrew is *chashah*. This word means to hush or to keep quiet, hold peace, keep silence, be silent and be still.

There are a number of reasons that God requires silence.

A. Reverence For His Presence and Word

In the natural world, when a king, a president or any other prominent figure or dignitary enters the company of others, there will, first of all, be some form of recognition and honor given to the person through clapping, bowing or other forms of expressions of honor. In contrast, when the VIP stands up to speak, a display of respect and reverence are expressed with an act of silence and stillness. How can we hear if we are not still to listen?

This principle works in the house of God as well as in our daily lives.

There are times that God wants us to be silent in honor and respect before Him in order that He may minister His words of life to us. Have you ever complained that you never hear from God? God is always speaking to us. He is the Word! Word speaks. However, is there ever stillness enough within our own beings to hear His voice? Do we calm down long enough to pause in respect and reverence to His majesty and simply allow Him to speak to our hearts?

In this age of modern technology, all manner of devices dominate our lives. Cell phones, I-pads, laptops, desktop computers, and an array of other gadgets fill our eyes and our ears with music, news, voices and sounds. Restaurant walls are loaded with TV screens which show a multitude of stations simultaneously. Our attention jumps from one sound to another, one picture to another, or one gadget to another. Do we even know how to be still anymore? People walk down the street, work out in the gym, drive their vehicles, and work their jobs, with earphones plugged into their ears. Our ears are continuously overloaded loaded with sounds. Few know how to turn the noise off and be still. Yet, we want to hear from God.

We need to open our ears and listen to the voice of our Lord.

Hold thy peace at the presence of the LORD... (Zephaniah 1:7)

But the LORD is in his holy temple: let all the earth keep silence before him. (Habakkuk 2:20)

Then a spirit passed before my face; the hair of my flesh stood up: It stood still but I could not discern the form thereof: an image was before mine eyes, there was silence, and I heard a voice saying, Shall mortal man be more just than God? shall a man be more pure than his maker? (Job 4:15-17) (Acts 15:12)

Here, we read that while Job was in total silence, he heard the voice of God's Spirit bring a word of rebuke and correction to him.

There is a power in the stillness and quietness of God's presence that cannot be experienced any other way, unless there is a total reverence and *hush* before the Lord.

And Moses said unto them, Stand still, and I will hear what the LORD will command concerning you. (Numbers 9:8)

B. Waiting on the Lord

Waiting on the Lord has to do with the receiving of revelation and the renewing of strength. Ministers, in particular, are guilty of always being *on the go*. I have been guilty of this very thing throughout the almost forty years that I have served God. Ministers can become so tired and run down that they become of little use to the church. To lead God's people on in progressive revelation and understanding, a leader has to withdraw him or herself, be still, and wait upon the LORD for renewed revelation, vision and strength.

But they that wait upon the LORD shall renew their strength; they shall mount up with wings as eagles; they shall run, and not be weary; they shall walk, and not faint. (Isaiah 40:31)

Keep silence *before me, O islands; and let the people renew their strength: let them come near; then let them speak: let us come near together to judgment. (Isaiah 41:1)*

God's people, particularly leaders and ministers, need to learn to retreat from the busy streets of service and ministry and renew their strength in silence and stillness before God. Ministers cannot lead people unless they take the time to be still and hear from God. We can only lead where we ourselves have walked.

Husbands, as the king, priest and prophet of their homes, have a spiritual responsibility to their families to lead them in the ways of the Lord. Do not get so wrapped up and overworked in trying to save the world that you do not have the time to wait upon the Lord concerning your own family. The reason that so many families, and churches, have unsolved and unresolved problems is because the spiritual head is too busy to take the time to wait on God and to be still before the LORD for answers.

C. See God Move

Doing a right thing, at the wrong time can get us into a lot of trouble. Praising, worshiping, singing, shouting, praying, or demonstrating God's powerful presence in some form or fashion are all good and right, as long as they are performed at the right place, in the right time and with the right spirit and the right motive. Doing any right and good deed at the wrong time can be a hindrance to God's will and plan. There are times that He calls for silence so that He can show Himself, speak His Word into our hearts and reveal His saving power and redemption.

And Moses said unto the people, Fear ye not, standstill, and see the salvation of the LORD, which he will shew to you today: for the Egyptians whom ye have seen today, ye shall see them again no more forever. The LORD shall fight for you, and ye shall hold your peace. (Exodus 14:13-14)

Moving when God tells us to move can accomplish great things for His Name's sake. But, moving in the flesh according to one's own will accomplishes nothing but death and destruction.

The story of the children of Israel at the edge of the Red Sea is a classic example of standing in silence and permitting God to move and to fight on behalf of His people. If the children of Israel had disobeyed God's command to stand still and had instead tried to fight against Pharaoh and his army themselves, they would have been defeated and destroyed. There are times that God wants us to realize that He can do it without us. There are times that He wishes to show us His mighty power as we stand aside, as it were, in reverence and honor to His great power and presence and allow God to be God.

125

Be still and know that I am God: (Psalm 46:10)

We should not be a hindrance to the way that God wants to move by acting in the flesh. There is a time for noise and active demonstrations, but there is a time for silence and stillness. As we grow in discernment, may we learn how to be balanced in all things before the Lord. God not only moves in and through noise, but He also moves through stillness and in a quiet whisper.

And he said, Go forth, and stand upon the mount before the LORD. And, behold, the LORD passed by, and a great and strong wind rent the mountains, and brake in pieces the rocks before the LORD; but the LORD was not in the wind: and after the wind an earthquake; but the LORD was not in the earthquake: And after the earthquake a fire: but the LORD was not in the fire: and after the fire a still small voice. (1 Kings 19:1142)

Just because there is shouting and active demonstration going on, it does not mean that God is in it. There is a time for boisterous rebuke, loud shouts of victorious praise, and active demonstrations of worship. In contrast, the small whisper can be just as powerful and the still small voice can render just as much a punch as the loud scream when God is in it.

There is great power in the whisper as well as in the shout. Find your balance. Allow God to be God!

D. Humility

Silence is also a demonstration or an act of humility.

The elders of the daughters of Zion sit upon the ground, and keep silence: they have cast up dust upon their heads; they have girded themselves with sackcloth: the virgins of Jerusalem hang down their heads to the ground. (Lamentations 2:10)

In this verse, the elders of the daughter of Zion sat on the ground (in the low place) and were in silence. Casting dust upon the head and being clothed with sackcloth were demonstrations of humbling oneself.

Chapter two of Lamentations is Jeremiah's lamentation concerning Jerusalem's misery due to God's hard dealings with her. The people became silent and humbled themselves before God. Often, in God's hard dealings with us, we are guilty of opening our mouths in complaint and speaking out of our ignorance concerning the way that God is handling things or the way that He is dealing with us. We need to learn to humble ourselves in these circumstances and be silent before the LORD and trust in His righteous dealings with us.

Why do we sit still? Assemble yourselves, and let us enter into the defenced cities, and let us be silent there: for the LORD our God hath put us to silence, and given us water of gall to drink, because we have sinned against the LORD. (Jeremiah 8:14)

Jesus is our defensed city. In Him, through Him and to Him we should humble ourselves in silence and rest in His eternal redemptive works in the midst of life's circumstances. Jesus, we love you. You are precious!

I trust that the lessons in this book will be a blessing to you as we, the body of Christ, endeavor to serve God in Spirit and in Truth.

But the hour cometh, and now is, when the true worshippers shall worship the Father in spirit and in truth: for the Father seeketh such to worship him. (John 4:23)

OTHER BOOK TITLES BY PAUL M HANSSEN:

- FROM UNDER THE TABLE
- DRESSING TO PLEASE THE LORD
- FOUNDATIONAL BIBLE STUDY GUIDE

ORDER FROM

www.sevenpillarschurch.com/resources